WARBIRDTECH
SERIES

VOLUME 22

DOUGLAS
A-26 INVADER

BY FREDERICK A. JOHNSEN

specialtypress
PUBLISHERS AND WHOLESALERS

Published by
Specialty Press Publishers and Wholesalers
11481 Kost Dam Road
North Branch, MN 55056
United States of America
(651) 583-3239

Distributed in the UK and Europe by
Airlife Publishing Ltd.
101 Longden Road
Shrewsbury
SY3 9EB
England

ISBN 1-58007-016-7

Designed by Dennis R. Jenkins

Printed in the United States of America

TABLE OF CONTENTS

THE DOUGLAS A-26 INVADER

PREFACE **4**
THANKS FOR HELPING TELL THE STORY

CHAPTER 1: A-26 DESIGN **5**
A SIMPLE PREMISE

CHAPTER 2: A-26 DEVELOPMENT **13**
A COMPLEX REALITY

CHAPTER 3: WORLD WAR TWO **25**
TRAINING AND DEPLOYMENT WITH THE A-26

CHAPTER 4: KOREA AND THE COLD WAR **37**
SOMETHING OLD, SOMETHING NEW

CHAPTER 5: PASSPORT TO POSTERITY **47**
A-26S IN FOREIGN USE

CHAPTER 6: SOUTHEAST ASIA **53**
A WAR OF ANACHRONISMS

SPECIAL FULL COLOR SECTION: INVADER COLOR **65**
SHADES OF A-26S

CHAPTER 7: CIVILIAN INVADERS **69**
BUSINESS SPEEDSHIPS AND FLYING FIRE ENGINES

CHAPTER 8: BOMBS ACROSS THE SEA **85**
BRITISH BOUNCING BOMB TESTED BY USAAF IN A-26

APPENDIX A **96**
USAAF/USAF INVADER UNITS

APPENDIX B **98**
ON MARK B-26 MODIFICATION PRICES—MAY 1962

SIGNIFICANT DATES **100**
KEY EVENTS IN THE HISTORY OF THE A-26 INVADER

PREFACE

Some aircraft deserve a measure of homage based on their aesthetics; others rate merit for longevity; and some purely by their performance. The racy Douglas A-26 Invader, veteran of three U.S. wars, rests securely in all three categories. Nurtured by famed designer Ed Heinemann and his team at Douglas Aircraft, the A-26 had good genes from the start. Douglas had a track record of reliable revenue-producing twin-engine airliners and the speedy art-deco A-20 Havoc attack bomber on which to draw experience.

And yet, reputation isn't everything. Design troubles with A-26 production early in its career caused delays that brought the ire of United States Army Air Forces chief Henry "Hap" Arnold. Complaints about lateral visibility over the huge engine nacelles, and awkward cockpit escape hatches, led to a substantial redesign of the Invader's canopy. A couple decades later, wing failures over Southeast Asia prompted concerns about structural strength, and gave rise to a beefy, much-modified variant, the K-model, prepared by On Mark Engineering.

A June 1948 nomenclature decision with unintended consequences saw the deletion of the attack category in U.S. Air Force terminology. With Martin B-26 Marauders retired from service by that time, A-26s were redesignated B-26s, to the confusion of many people ever since. Still later, in the 1960s, the designation of B-26Ks based in

Thailand was changed to A-26A, in a sense bringing the Invader full circle.

Fire bomber operators in the United States and Canada used numerous surplus A-26s; executive conversions were produced; and the Air National Guard as well as foreign governments armed themselves with A-26s for years after World War Two.

If the Douglas A-26 endured occasional criticisms, its accomplishments more than made up for the few drawbacks. And the Invader's many crews over the decades of its service deserve acknowledgment for taking the A-26 on harrowing sorties in the face of daunting obstacles—man-made and natural.

Thanks are due to those who helped tell this story of Douglas' sleek attack bomber. They include: Aero Trader (Carl Scholl and Tony Ritzman), the Air Force Historical Research Agency, Peter M. Bowers, Harry Gann (and the considerable Douglas company archives he protected for so many years), the Malcolm Gougon collection, Dan Hagedorn, Ben Howser, Kenneth G. Johnsen, Don Keller (Air Depot), Keith Laird, Bob Mikesh, Milo Peltzer, the San Diego Aerospace Museum (and Ray Wagner and library staff), and Ken Shake.

The availability of Invaders during the Cold War has made them pivotal aspects in two books of particular note. Authors Dan Hagedorn and Leif Hellstrom have amassed

the definitive work on Cold War Invaders in their volume, *Foreign Invaders: The Douglas Invader in Foreign Military and U.S. Clandestine Service*, from Specialty Press. Col. Michael E. Haas, USAF (Ret), weaves an intriguing story of cloak-and-dagger operations, often involving B-26s, in his study, *Apollo's Warriors—United States Air Force Special Operations during the Cold War*, published by Air University Press and the U.S. Government Printing Office.

One note of caution when viewing photos of A-26s: The gun nose and Plexiglas nose, hallmarks of the B- and C-models, respectively, were readily interchangeable. This led to a number of Invaders with tail numbers indicating one variant, while the nose configuration was of another model. Some historians suggest the swapping of noses was tantamount to changing the model; other authors have retained the aircraft's model identity as built, regardless of subsequent nose-swaps.

We would not have the Douglas Invader to treat in the Warbird Tech Series were it not for the people who actually created A-26s during World War Two, and who crewed and maintained them for decades to follow. Let this volume be a respectful acknowledgment of their efforts.

Frederick A. Johnsen
1998

A-26 DESIGN

Douglas designer Edward H. Heinemann honed his skills working with other greats of the industry, including the often unorthodox wizard Jack Northrop. His work with Northrop served to define Ed Heinemann's own design philosophy, which he was proud to call conservative. But it was a conservatism borne of knowledge, not fear of the unknown. Ed Heinemann tended to shun gimmicks, but the way he amalgamated design elements was as practical as it was poetic. Already the patent holder of record for the Douglas A-20, Ed Heinemann paid a visit to Wright Field on a snowy winter trip in 1940 where he heard about the Army's desire to supersede the A-20 with a bomber yet more capable. (Douglas historian Harry Gann says a variation on the A-26 genesis story has engineer/artist R.G. Smith and engineering vice president Arthur Raymond hatching a major follow-on to the A-20 at about the same time. Gann said Smith recalled working over the Christmas holidays laying out a proposal. In his autobiography, Heinemann said other Douglas officials, including Raymond, knew of the Army's interest in a follow-on to the A-20. Obviously, the development of a major aircraft requires the ideas and work of more than one person.)

During his wintry Wright Field session, Heinemann listened to his military host, and jotted a list of desired performance traits for the new bomber beside a similar list

for the existing A-20. High on the Army's list was installation of a 75-mm cannon, as was being proposed for the B-25 as well. Some at Douglas thought the A-20 could accommodate the big gun; Heinemann argued successfully that the narrow fuselage of the A-20 was reason enough to devise a new, more capacious, bomber to carry the cannon, its ammunition, and a cannoneer. Even as Heinemann and his associates at Douglas' El Segundo, California, plant began fleshing out a 75-mm gun variant of the new bomber, a nightfighter version, with four ventral 20-mm cannons and four .50-caliber machine guns in a remotely controlled rear turret, was created on paper.[1]

In a 5 November 1940 letter to Douglas Aircraft, Maj. Frank O. Carroll, chief of the Air Corps' Experimental Engineering Section at Wright Field, summed a list of A-20 traits deemed insufficient when "viewed in the light of the present war in Europe." In the absence of a complete Air Corps design specification for the new bomber, Major Carroll offered, in the interim, five areas of the A-20 needing improvement in any new design:

"a. No interchangeability of crew. This is generally considered the most serious of all.

b. Insufficient defensive armament. Guns should be in powered turrets for all around defense. .50 caliber guns preferable, if not mandatory, and ammunition supplies should be increased.

c. The design strength of 6.00 G ultimate which is reduced to 5.5 G when the gross weight is increased by modernization is too little for safety in the maneuvers now contemplated. Shallow glide bombing will be attempted with the A-20B,

Wooden wind tunnel model of the XA-26 in 1/20 scale differed but little from Invader as built. Large prop spinners of a handful of X-variant Invaders were soon discarded on production A-26s. (U.S. Air Force)

XA-26 in flight showed essential form of the series. Opaque canopy hatch may be airbrush censorship. (Douglas via Peter M. Bowers)

but there is no possibility of accomplishing a moderate form of dive bomber attack which the Chief of the Air Corps has repeatedly asked for in this type.

d. Landing and takeoff distances are considered too great for close support airplane, which is required to operate from relatively unimproved fields within 100 miles of the ground forces.

e. Speed now considered excellent for this size and type, but it will probably have to be increased for airplanes to be produced in 1942-43, particularly the speed at intermediate altitude."[2]

For Ed Heinemann, the XA-26 was a chance to rectify some deficiencies of the older A-20 design. A new aluminum-alloy, 75S, was incorporated because it promised considerable weight savings. If this seemed contrary to Heinemann's legendary conservatism, it was his engineering savvy that ensured the new high-temper metal was shaped and employed in ways that would not concentrate stresses to its detriment. From the National Advisory Committee for Aeronautics (NACA) came a recommended laminar-flow airfoil that promised greater speed, and demanded smooth skin surfaces.[3]

Intended from the outset as a fresh design with which to replace the B-25 and Martin B-26, the Douglas A-26 concept was shared with NACA engineers in early 1941. NACA had earned a reputation for devising streamlining and propulsion advantages for American aircraft. In the case of the XA-26, two issues were raised with the engineers of NACA: Correct fuselage cross-section for the A-26, and engine nacelle dimensions.

NACA head mechanical engineer Elton W. Miller described the proposed XA-26: "It is powered by two 2800 engines in nacelles which extend especially far forward with respect to the wing. The nacelles are below the wing, the upper surface being tangent with the upper surface of the wing. The nacelles appear unusually long."[4]

Miller wrote in a 1941 NACA memo: "With reference to the length of the nacelle, it appeared that the length was determined by the position of the propellers with reference to the pilot's cockpit and the personnel quarters in the fuselage and by the space needed for retracting the

XA-26B, fitted with huge 75-mm cannon in the right side of the nose where its operation and loading would not interfere with the pilot, was not destined to be the definitive Invader. Streamlined "bullet-nose" over cannon muzzle was experimental fairing designed to blow open when the gun was fired; tried also on cannon-armed B-25s, this fairing was subsequently discarded. (Peter M. Bowers)

landing gear. It did not appear possible to make it any shorter for practical reasons and nobody suggested making it any longer. It was the general opinion that the drag of the nacelle would depend largely on the skin friction and more especially on the number of scoops and other protuberances on the surface." NACA engineer E.N. Jacobs told the gathering of Douglas, military, and NACA specialists that nacelles this large would constitute a considerable percentage of the total drag of the A-26. Jacobs opined that if the engines could be buried in the fuselage, and use shafts and gears to drive the pro-

XA-26 evidently had an identity crisis, as these photos show tail number 219504 (representing 42-19504) when its serial is listed as 41-19504. (Douglas via Peter M. Bowers)

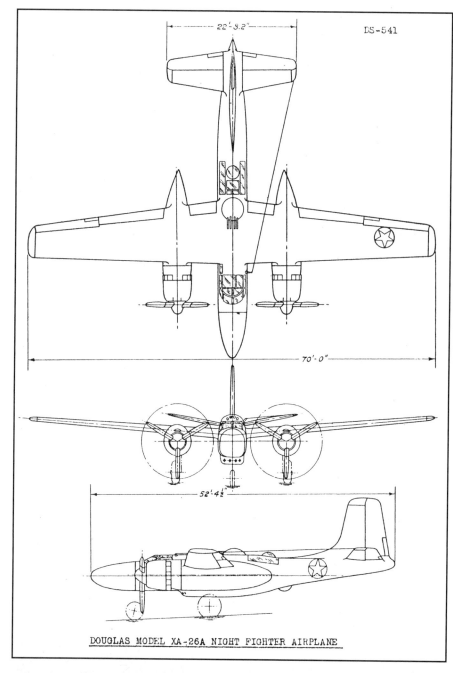

22'-9.2"

DS-941

70'-0"

52'-4½"

DOUGLAS MODEL XA-26A NIGHT FIGHTER AIRPLANE

Early Douglas line drawing depicted XA-26A night fighter with a large four-gun top turret in the fashion of the P-61 Black Widow; four guns also were fixed to fire forward in a ventral bulge where the bomb bay would be on bomber versions. Interestingly, this aircraft retained its A-for-Attack designation and was only distinguished by the suffix model letter 'A', unlike night fighter versions of the A-20 which received the nomenclature P-70. Large hemispheric sighting blisters were incorporated on the night fighter Invader. (Douglas/Harry Gann)

pellers, considerable drag reduction might be expected. Dr. M.U. Clauser, representing Douglas Aircraft, was reported by Miller as thinking it was very unlikely that any manufacturer would be willing to proceed with such a radical design during emergency times such as the uncertainties of 1941.[5] (Nonetheless, by 1944 Douglas Aircraft flew a new bomber, the XB-42, which employed this philosophy, using shafts to transmit power from two buried Allison V-1710-125 engines to contra-rotating pusher propellers at the extreme aft end of the fuselage. The XB-42 enjoyed exceptionally high speed for a bomber, in excess of 450 miles an hour. The XB-42 helped usher out the propeller era; a jet offshoot, the XB-43, ultimately was bypassed by more promising jet bomber designs.)[6]

139108

A-26B-5-DL in natural metal finish showed the bulged nose containing a 75-mm cannon. Direction-finding loop radio antenna is located aft of dorsal gunner's glazing on this and other early B-models. (Douglas/Harry Gann)

WARBIRDTECH
S E R I E S

Miller described the XA-26 fuselage discussion: "The main question seemed to be whether it would be better to use a square-section fuselage as contemplated in the preliminary design or whether a circular fuselage would be more efficient." A circular fuselage, he noted, would need to be larger to accommodate the useful volume of the square. Any theoretical advantages to a circular shape were put in doubt by another drag-inducing phenomenon noted in earlier tests of circular versus narrow fuselages: "… It was the general opinion that the intersection of the wing with the fuselage tended to overcome the difference between the two shapes and that as the square fuselage had rounded corners, there would be little to choose between the two."[7]

During this meeting, the engineers discussed Douglas Aircraft's intentions of conducting routine wind tunnel tests with a 1/8-scale model at the California Institute of Technology (Caltech) in Pasadena, California; in-depth wind tunnel testing in NACA's 19-foot tunnel for the purpose of studying laminar flow, flaps, longitudinal stability, stalling, and other questions; tests of a large (possibly full-size) nacelle to verify engine cooling capability; and tests of several large-scale wings in the NACA low-turbulence tunnel. [8]

Douglas' design team set out to make the A-26 easy to produce (although milling machine shortages stubbed this initially). As an example, the quick-change power-plant packages were designed to

Instrument panel of night fighter XA-26A showed single-pilot arrangement, with small radar scope visible near upper right horn of bowtie-style control yoke. (U.S. Air Force, T.C. Weaver, and Peter M. Bowers)

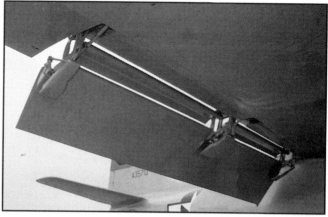

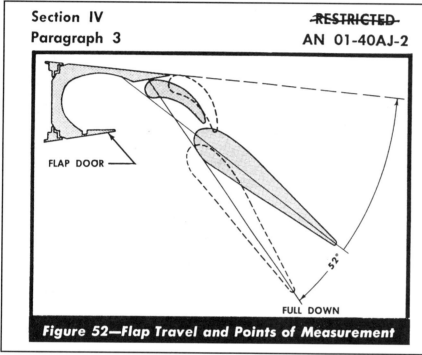

FLAP DOOR

52°

FULL DOWN

Figure 52—Flap Travel and Points of Measurement

The A-26's sophisticated wing flaps used airflow deflectors, as depicted in an erection and maintenance manual, to increase efficiency.

26. Ed Heinemann said the engines of the A-26 "are cooled with the latest type high entrance velocity cowling developed by the National Advisory Committee for Aeronautics and the Douglas company. This cowling not only has less aerodynamic resistance but has resulted in lower engine temperatures than heretofore experienced."[11] The A-26 demonstrably pushed the state of the art forward in many design and performance areas.

Futuristic Flaps

interchange left or right as needed.[9] Decades later, these quick-change A-26 engine packages would find another home on the first iteration of Canadair CL-215 purpose-built amphibious water bombers.

Ultimately, Douglas created a one-third scale model of the A-26 engine nacelle with an electric motor turning a scale propeller for use in the Caltech wind tunnel. Running water cooled the motor, and the surrounding city of Pasadena complained about the volume of water the tests were consuming. Ed Heinemann recalled later that a switch to noc-

turnal testing of the nacelle seemed to quell the city's objections. Heinemann persuaded NACA's Dr. Carl Lewis to go contrary to the NACA practice of building its own wind tunnel models, to allow Douglas to make a big 10-foot wingspan A-26 for further testing at Langley. The outcome of all this wind tunnel testing was a remarkably refined design. Early flights by AAF fliers including tester Col. Stan Umstead prompted positive reviews.[10]

The cowling at the front of each nacelle did more than merely shroud the R-2800 engines of the A-

Among the innovations designed into the A-26 was a flap design that used multiple airfoil shaped panels to optimum advantage. In a 1943 memorandum, designer Heinemann described the "Douglas slotted wing flap" which he said produced a 30 percent higher lift coefficient than did the flaps of the older A-20 aircraft. "This flap is superior to the well known Fowler flap since it has a lower pitching moment for a given lift coefficient," Heinemann explained.[12]

A wartime Douglas article said: "The use of the recently designed and

Silver A-26B shows lopsided size of canopy overhead hatches. The loop antenna on this aircraft, still located behind the gunner's dorsal window, has been enclosed in a streamlined teardrop housing. Anti-glare paint covers inside upper quarters of large nacelles forward of the wings, as well as curving on the top of the nose ahead of the windscreen.
(Douglas/Harry Gann)

A-26C phantom drawing shows bulging late-style canopy, and placement of the two power turrets.
(Douglas/Harry Gann)

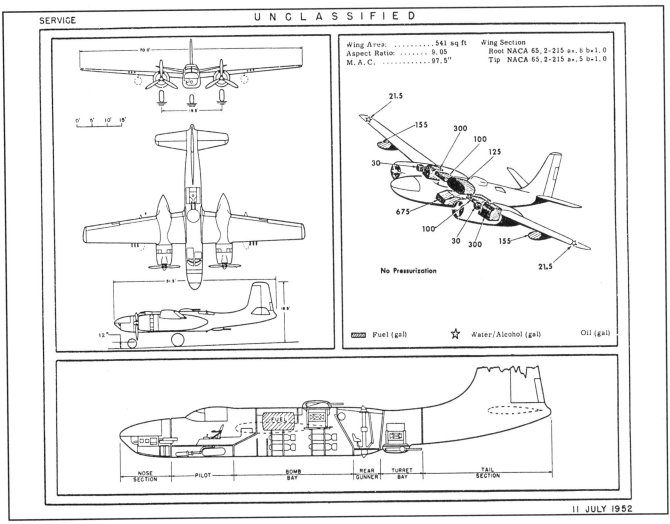

SERVICE

U N C L A S S I F I E D

Wing Area: .... 541 sq ft
Aspect Ratio: 9.05
M.A.C. ....97.5"

Wing Section
Root NACA 65,2-215 a=.8 b=1.0
Tip NACA 65,2-215 a=.5 b=1.0

No Pressurization

Fuel (gal)   Water/Alcohol (gal)   Oil (gal)

NOSE SECTION | PILOT | BOMB BAY | REAR GUNNER | TURRET BAY | TAIL SECTION

11 JULY 1952

At least 15 Invader fuselages stretched into the distance at Long Beach as workers made them into complete bombers. Lengthy serial numbers taxed the available space on fixed vertical fins; AAF procedure called for keeping the numbers off the movable—and readily replaceable—rudders. (McDonnell Douglas via Harry Gann)

wind tunnel tested Douglas High Lift Wing Flap on the A-26 permits higher wing loading while maintaining take-off and landing characteristics which are superior to the performance of former models. The use of this new flap in lieu of flaps previously used permits a 10 percent slower landing speed. In addition, the take-off is greatly improved due to the low drag and high lift characteristics of the new flap."[13]

Easy Access

Ed Heinemann's design for the Douglas Skyraider single-engine attack aircraft included deliberate thought on streamlining the maintenance process. This showed up in Heinemann's A-26 scheme as well. A wartime Douglas document noted: "To facilitate assembly, service and repair under the most adverse conditions, simplicity, and accessibility

have been considered throughout the entire design of the A-26. Realizing that battles may be won or lost by time spent in service or repair, labor and time-saving ideas have been incorporated wherever possible." As an example of this, the Douglas paper said, "All electric lines and plumbing fixtures are installed so that they may be serviced and repaired by merely removing a portion of the fuselage skin."[14]

[1] Edward H. Heinemann and Rosario Rausa, *Ed Heinemann — Combat Aircraft Designer,* Naval Institute Press, Annapolis, Maryland, 1980. [2] Letter, Maj. Frank O. Carroll, Air Corps, to Douglas Aircraft Co.,"Research and Development,"5 November 1940. [3] Edward H. Heinemann and Rosario Rausa, *Ed Heinemann — Combat Aircraft Designer,* Naval Institute Press, Annapolis, Maryland, 1980. [4] Memorandum for Engineer-In-Charge, by Elton W. Miller (NACA head mechanical engineer),"Conference with representatives of the Douglas Company and the Army Liaison Office on the XA-26 airplane," 7 February 1941. [5] *Ibid.* [6] Lloyd S. Jones, *U.S. Bombers — 1928 to 1980s,* Aero Publishers, Fallbrook, California, 1980. [7] Memorandum for Engineer-In-Charge, by Elton W. Miller (NACA head mechanical engineer),"Conference with representatives of the Douglas Company and the Army Liaison Office on the XA-26 airplane," 7 February 1941. [8] *Ibid.* [9] "Case History of A-26 Airplane," compiled by Historical Division, Intelligence, T-2, Air Technical Service Command, Wright Field, Oct 1945. [10] Edward H. Heinemann and Rosario Rausa, *Ed Heinemann — Combat Aircraft Designer,* Naval Institute Press, Annapolis, Maryland, 1980. [11] Memorandum, E.H. Heinemann to A.M. Rochlen, *et al,* "Model A-26 Publicity,"15 April 1943. [12] *Ibid.* [13] Bob Knight,"The A-26 — Douglas Invader," September 1942, revised April 1944, (Douglas archives via Harry Gann). [14] *Ibid.*

A-26 DEVELOPMENT

It was faster than some fighters, and yet was a twin-engine bomber with a gross weight of 26,700 pounds. The A-26 Invader sprang from the innovative design team headed by Ed Heinemann at Douglas Aircraft. Heinemann brought good credentials to give the A-26 a fine pedigree; other Douglas products bearing the Heinemann touch included the SBD Dauntless, A-20 Havoc, and, later, the AD Skyraider and A-4 Skyhawk, among others. But the A-26 was not without flaws in its execution, and production delays infuriated United States Army Air Forces chief Gen. Henry H. "Hap" Arnold.

Genesis for the A-26 came about in November 1940 as the Air Corps' Experimental Engineering Section at Wright Field assimilated data about European combat aircraft, and concluded the A-20 could not be expected to keep pace. Marching orders for Douglas designers assigned to the new bomber project were that the aircraft must be faster, with greater defensive armament, have greater design strength, and use less runway for takeoffs and landings than did the A-20. The Air Corps harbored the hope—realized after the end of World War Two—that the new Douglas bomber would effectively replace the B-25 and Martin B-26 Marauder in service.[1]

The process of creating a viable combat aircraft has long been studied and modified with the intent of abbreviating the time between inception and operation. If the time

from concept to production can be shortened, this may result in economies for the manufacturer. And the military would gladly field a new aircraft as soon as possible, especially if war clouds are on the horizon. In this setting, according to an Air Force study of the A-26 project, "Douglas proposed ... to schedule such a thorough series of wind tunnel tests of the experi-

mental models that mass production could follow almost immediately."[2] This idea came in an era when the manufacturers did much more developmental testing of their own products; in the decades after World War Two, developmental testing increasingly was shared with the Air Force.

In a quirky statistic, the experimental engineering section at Wright Field noted in February 1941, and an Air Force report later relayed, that "a comparison of prices indicated that the price per pound of the XA-26 was greater than that of any other experimental model listed." Attempts to get Douglas to lower the per-pound price were unsuccessful, but the Wright Field

engineers did acknowledge "that the price per pound for the XA-26 and XA-26A airplanes was partially justified by the fact that the XA-26A was radically different from the XA-26, so that Douglas was, in effect, quoting on design and construction of two different airplanes."[3]

Some A-26Bs used staggered six-gun .50-caliber nose, plus six internal wing guns. Though it could be towed by its nosewheel strut, the A-26 experienced some problems with nose gear, and pilots were cautioned not to perform engine run-ups with the nose wheel cocked to one side. (Bowers collection)

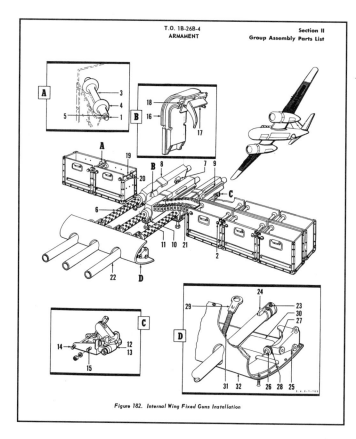

Figure 182. Internal Wing Fixed Guns Installation

Fed by a train of micarta ammunition boxes, three internal A-26 wing .50-caliber M-2 machine guns were staggered to accommodate ammunition feed paths, as shown in an A-26 illustrated parts book. Blast tubes covered the muzzles of the guns. Item 16 in detail 'B' is a chute for ammunition link ejection.

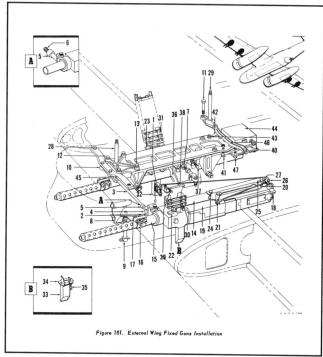

Figure 181. External Wing Fixed Guns Installation

Some A-26s mounted as many as eight .50-caliber wing guns in pods that paired the weapons. Underwing A-26 guns were mounted on their sides.

In the latter part of April 1941, mock-up inspections of the new Douglas bomber were made. Following contract negotiations, on 2 June 1941 contract number W535 ac-17946 was issued for the purchase of one XA-26 attack aircraft and one XA-26A night fighter at an estimated price of $2,083,385.79 plus a fee of just over $125,000. Shortly thereafter a change order was introduced authorizing an additional aircraft, the XA-26B, to be fitted with a 75-mm cannon. Douglas had originally submitted a higher contract amount, based on a fixed price that effectively pinned Douglas to that amount even if costs ran higher. A lesser amount was negotiated by changing the contract to a cost-plus-fixed-fee basis, which was more palatable to Douglas.

By the end of October 1941, the first production contract for 500 A-26s was let. Meanwhile, availability of some components for the prototypes was delayed, causing some schedule slips. At Wright Field, the Production Engineering Section pored over the evidently versatile A-26 design and contemplated varied roles for the new attack bomber, including medium altitude bombardment with a bombardier nose; tank busting and ground attack with a 75-mm cannon or four 37-mm cannons; ground attack with six .50-caliber machine guns in the nose; nightfighting with radar; and reconnaissance and photography with long-range gasoline tanks.[4]

Early in May 1942, Douglas informed the AAF that the delivery

schedule for A-26s would necessarily slip because delays encountered with the prototype would also affect production deliveries. An Air Force study noted: "Inability to obtain landing gear struts had necessitated revising the first flight date from 15 January 1942 to 1 July 1942. Other delays in delivery of self-sealing tanks, turrets, and GFE (government-furnished equipment) items such as engines, propellers, spinners, and generators were adversely affecting the A-26 program. Complete engineering information on turrets to be installed was not completed until 2 May 1942."[5]

By the summer of 1942, the AAF opted to build the first 500 A-26s with the 75-mm cannon nose, and make 200 gun noses with six .50-

When the U.S. Navy expressed interest in the Douglas Invader, this A-26C example, assigned Navy BuAer no. 57990, was designated XJD-1. (U.S. Navy via Peter M. Bowers)

calibers as alternates for installation in the field. (Ultimately, the 75-mm proposal, to be housed in a wooden nose, would fall out of favor.) Meanwhile, first flight of the XA-26 occurred on 10 July 1942. By that time, estimated date of first production A-26s was July 1943. Creation of production tooling was taking longer than anticipated; the first six production A-26s were now set to be built using prototype tooling as a stopgap measure. The AAF's Production Division at Wright Field directed Douglas Aircraft to

reassign at least two-thirds of the personnel then on the huge C-74 transport program to the A-26; tooling engineers were especially coveted. Transports took another hit from the AAF in the interest of accelerating A-26 production when, according to a study of the A-26, "no engineers were to be utilized in improving crew comfort or arrangement in cargo planes unless specifically authorized by Wright Field." Further mutations of A-26 armament packages were to be shelved "until a more advanced

stage of production had been reached." In 1942, priorities for the A-26 were set to be: 75-mm version, bombardier/observer nose, and machine gun nose. [6]

The AAF began moving away from early ideas for using multiple 37-mm cannons in A-26s. As late as September 1942, Douglas was considering a four-gun 37-mm nose, and a two-gun external 37-mm rack to be mounted beneath the bomb bay. By December of that year, Douglas was told by the AAF

U.S. Navy JD-1D at Point Mugu with early forward-hinging canopy shows specialized Plexiglas nose cap, different from bombardier-nosed A-26Cs. JD-1s could launch Ryan Firebee drones; drop tank on opposite wing station provided ballast. (U.S. Navy via Peter M. Bowers)

cannon beneath the bomb bay of a B-25 airplane had produced serious damage to the nose wheel doors and skin structure."[7]

In January 1943, despite the efforts to throw more skilled workers into the A-26 program, Douglas told the USAAF at Wright Field that design changes and tooling problems made it inevitable that production A-26s would slip back to October of that year. So keen was the AAF on getting A-26s into production that Douglas was authorized that month to delay engineering schedules on other Army Air Forces projects in order to speed up delivery of A-26s. While Douglas wrestled with delays on its original Long Beach A-26 production order, a second contract was let on 17 March 1943 for 500 A-26Bs with the 75-mm cannon, to be built at Douglas' Tulsa, Oklahoma, facility. Though still clinging to the big gun as the desired armament for the first 1,000 A-26s, planners canceled the proposed four-gun 37-mm installation the following August.

to curtail armament studies, other than the 75-mm nose, until the A-26 reached a more advanced stage of production, although some 37-mm options were reserved for later exploration. By late December 1942, Douglas was proceeding with design of an all-purpose gun nose, intended to mount a variety of weapons in several combinations, changeable in the field by installing different guns in brackets in the common nose. The arrays of firepower envisioned for this nose included six .50-caliber machine guns; four .50-caliber machine guns and one 37-mm T-20

cannon; two 37-mm T-20 cannons; or two .50-caliber machine guns and one 75-mm cannon. (In practice, .50-caliber machine guns became the weapons of choice for the A-26, ranging from a successful eight-gun solid nose to a glass nose with provision for fixed .50-calibers to the side.) Then, abruptly in February 1943, according to an AAF study, the Engineering Division at Wright Field "informed Douglas that no further study was to be made of the installation of the 37-mm high velocity cannon under the bomb bay of the A-26. Firing tests of the installation of a 37-mm

Even as deliveries began in the fall of 1943, proposals for changes were hoisted aloft, to the potential degra-

dation of the schedule. Flight controls for a second pilot were considered—the earlier A-20 Havoc had a narrow cockpit only wide enough for a single pilot, but the A-26 could accommodate two side by side. By the spring of 1944, a shortage of machinery for making A-26 wing spars was slowing the program badly. It was ironic that the design seemed sound and in need of little change, but the manufacturing was a bottleneck.[8] AAF chief Gen. Hap Arnold sent an unvarnished letter to Gen. Oliver Echols with instructions to give General Arnold a workable plan for producing A-26s. General Arnold alluded to problems producing B-29s at Wichita (sometimes called the "Battle of Kansas"). Clearly, problems in production of these two bombers weighed heavily on Hap Arnold.[9]

General Arnold elaborated: "We cannot have more A-26s although we have plenty of fuselages, but not enough wings. We could build more wings if we had more spars, but we cannot build more spars due to difficult output of machinery. We might be able to build more wings if we were able to get more machinery, but whether we will be able to get more machinery I was unable to determine and nobody could give me the answer. *One thing is certain: I want the A-26s for use in this war and not for the next war. If something drastic is not done, we cannot hope to replace the B-25s, B-26s and A-20s with the A-26.*" (Emphasis added.)

The seemingly endless production capacity of American industry was hobbled in early 1944, as far as A-26 wing spar production was concerned, by a finite number of milling machines in the nation capable of handling Invader spars. According to Maj. Gen. Oliver Echols, busy birddogging the A-26 production problems, consideration was given to using mills at Boeing in Seattle and Wichita, and Bell at Marietta, Georgia, to make A-26 spars "until such time as the machines ordered for the A-26 program are delivered." Beech, in line to make spars for the Tulsa A-26 order, awaited delivery of its machinery.[10]

According to a study made by the AAF in 1945: "Through March 1944, wing spar caps had been the gov-

Both sides of a Navy JD-1D assigned to squadron VU-3 shows suspension of target drone and ballast tank. (E.M. Sommerich via Peter M. Bowers)

Testbed for a Navy ramjet drone project, circa November 1946, this A-26C once sparked rumors of a crash when the rocket it carried was ignited as the A-26 flew out of Muroc Army Air Base over the desert town of Boron, California, with smoke and flame issuing from the ramjet. Engineer Don Thomson recalled the noise of the ramjet could be heard over the A-26's engine sounds in the gunner's compartment where he rode to operate the rocket. The A-26 ramjet testbed carried a sign denoting Pilotless Aircraft Unit—Naval Air Station Mojave, California. (Don Thomson and Peter M. Bowers collections)

erning factor in the production of A-26 airplanes." The wing of the A-26 was "entirely different from that of any other airplane," an Air Force report noted. "It (the A-26 wing) incorporates eight inboard and eight outboard spars. Each of the eight outboard spars was different from the others and required a special machine arrangement."

Even though the outward appearance of the Invader changed little over its production life, at one point as many as 35 change orders were received in a day on the aircraft, with resulting delays. The failure of an A-26B wing during static tests in May 1944 prompted a request from the AAF that Douglas redesign the structure, to increase the wing's strength by 10 percent. Seven static wing failures, even after fixes had been applied, led to the request for substantial redesign.[11]

The operational deployment of four A-26s with Fifth Air Force in the Pacific in July 1944 gave vital feedback. (See also Chapter Three.) The initial combat Invaders were called unsatisfactory because of insufficient lateral visibility for the pilot which made low-level attack formations dangerous. Far East Air Forces commander Gen. George Kenney was quoted as saying: "We do not want the A-26 under any circumstances as a replacement for

anything." The AAF Production Division at Wright Field essentially concurred with the general. But in Europe, Ninth Air Force commander Gen. Hoyt Vandenberg remained interested in replacing B-26s and A-20s with the new Invaders.[12]

Where early A-26s had a cockpit canopy flush with the top contour of the fuselage, a new, slightly raised canopy was created to enhance pilot visibility over the huge engine nacelles to either side of the fuselage. When the Douglas Tulsa factory said the new canopy could not be incorporated earlier than January 1945, General Arnold said it could be done more quickly. The AAF noted Douglas had its strong engineering talent in California; unless better liaison could be worked out between the Douglas California Invader assembly line and the Tulsa line, Tulsa could expect to lag in its incorporation of modifications like the improved canopy. (The concentration of engineering talent in California continued to be a source of concern; as late as March 1945, Douglas was moving personnel from Tulsa to Long Beach to give them access to A-26 detail information, while sending a Long Beach engineer to Tulsa to help explain data received there.) Two more Invader contracts, approved in December 1944, added 2,400 aircraft to the production run; supplements to the contracts later added 1,600 more Invaders to the orders, including 350 to be delivered as A-26Ds with improved powerplants. By May 1945, with war in Europe over, these contracts were reduced, or sometimes terminated outright, taking with them all but the first A-26D as well as thousands of Invaders of earlier types.

On 9 January 1945, the AAF's Procurement Division at Wright Field learned that Douglas wanted to halt A-26 deliveries until several power-plant rework items could be completed. The changes incorporated by Douglas diminished the possibility of fire and reduced the likelihood of engine cut-out during take-off. With AAF approval, Douglas took time to introduce the changes, and in remarkably short order, the California A-26 line resumed deliveries on 12 January while the Tulsa, Oklahoma line resumed deliveries the following day.

In early 1945, A-26s in combat were getting mixed reviews. Maj. Gen. S. E. Anderson of the Ninth Bombardment Division reported that pilots considered the Invader better than any aircraft they had flown, once they got used to it. Even General Kenney had some praise for the A-26; an AAF history said, "the version with the eight-gun nose and

Recontoured to provide inlet and exhaust for a General Electric I-16 (J-31) jet engine in the fuselage, and flown part of its life with four-blade propellers, the sole XA-26F was photographed 15 November 1945. R-2800-83 piston engines were fitted. The boosted bomber averaged 413 miles per hour in June 1946 over a course of more than 620 miles. (Douglas/Harry Gann)

The cockpit of a dual-control B-26C (radio call sign 35634), fitted with new control yokes in the style of On Mark B-26Ks. In fact, this Invader was upgraded to K-model configuration and reserialled 64-17670. (Bowers collection)

no bottom turret had proved to be highly satisfactory as a replacement for A-20s and B-25s" in Far East Air Forces usage. But gremlins lingered, especially with nose gear problems, canopy frosting, and brake write-ups.[13]

By April 1945, according to an AAF A-26 compilation: "Due to the reduced demand for bombardier nose A-26 airplanes for use in the ETO and to the expected employment of A-26 airplanes in Pacific areas, A-26 airplanes were to be produced in a ratio of [two-thirds] gun noses to [one-third] bombardier noses." A planning memorandum to the AAF, dated 16 May 1945, and reflecting Allied victory in Europe, said requirements for A-26s were to be based upon assumptions including: Seven A-26 groups, including one Pathfinder group, were to be redeployed to the Pacific; all medium and light bomb groups already arrayed against Japan, except for three FEAF B-25 units, were to re-equip with A-26s; no A-26s were to be

offered up for Lend-Lease; and A-26s would replace other B-26 units by attrition beginning in June 1946. Based on these and other assumptions, it was deemed appropriate to curtail A-26 production to 150 aircraft per month.[14] Not produced in quantities as high as some of the bombers it was ultimately to replace, the sophisticated A-26 had an average unit cost of $254,624 in the hectic, pre-operational year 1943; dropping to $192,457 for 1944, and ending production at an average cost of $175,892 in 1945. By comparison, B-25s were averaging $116,752 for 1945. Martin B-26 Marauders, whose acceptances dwindled by 1945, were nearly as costly as A-26s for 1944, coming in at an average price of $192,427 in that year.[15]

By June 1945, production of Invaders had been terminated by the AAF at Tulsa with aircraft number 1753, while the plant at Long Beach continued to work on A-26s. A-26 contracts were terminated entirely on 27 August 1945, with the formal surrender of Japan only days away.[16]

A-26s were involved in tests which created a night photo reconnaissance variant (FA-26), a jet-augmented version (XA-26F), a night intruder, and a tow target aircraft. Douglas Aircraft even proposed a postwar model, the A-26Z, which would be built with the elevated canopy, a rearranged cockpit layout, crew entry through the nosewheel well, and droppable gasoline tanks on the wingtips. The AAF's Air

**SECTION II
GROUP ASSEMBLY PARTS LIST**

INDEX NUMBERS		FIGURE NUMBERS	INDEX NUMBERS		FIGURE NUMBERS
1	SYSTEM GROUP	5-80	7	POWER PLANT	109
2	MAIN LANDING GEAR	81-82	8	WING STRUCTURE	110-116
3	NOSE GEAR	83-85	9	EMPENNAGE	117-120
4	FUSELAGE FURNISHINGS	86-89	10	FUSELAGE STRUCTURE	121-132
5	ARMAMENT EQUIPMENT	90-99	11	EXTERNAL MARKINGS	133
6	RECONNAISSANCE EQUIPMENT	100-108	12	SPECIAL SUPPORT EQUIPMENT	134-135
				SPECIAL SERVICE TOOLS	136

Figure 1. Major Assembly Breakdown

2-1

Technical Service Command (ATSC) acknowledged improvements in this Douglas proposal, but said the service had no requirement for such an aircraft.

B-26K Counter Invader

Already established as a refurbisher of plush executive transport A-26s since the 1950s, in 1963, On Mark Engineering in Van Nuys, California, produced the ultimate A-26, initially as the B-26K Counter Invader,

later redesignated A-26A. Taking a stock Invader in October 1962, the small On Mark organization produced the YB-26K in time to fly on 28 January 1963. The 40 production B-26Ks which followed were given new serials, from 64-17640 through 64-17679.

The On-Mark Counter Invader featured strengthened wings with eight specially designed hardpoints that could carry a variety of stores with a total weight of 8,000

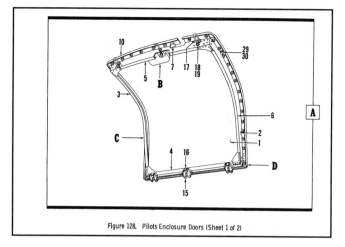

Figure 128. Pilots Enclosure Doors (Sheet 1 of 2)

(Left) Clamshell overhead pilot's hatch hinged outward on later, raised Invader canopies.

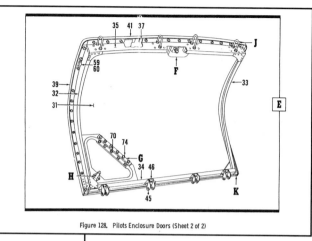

Figure 128. Pilots Enclosure Doors (Sheet 2 of 2)

(Above) Late style clamshell canopy hatch over the right side of cockpit was longer than counterpart on the left side, just as early-style glazing had been more extensive over right half of cockpit.

pounds. The Air Force said the B-26K could carry a "maximum disposable armament" weight of about 12,000 pounds (other accounts say 11,000 pounds), including fuselage bomb bay capacity of up to 4,000 pounds. For extra range or loitering time, each wing's inboard pylon could carry a 230-gallon drop tank instead of bombs or rockets. Machine gun packages could also be slung from the pylons, although the eight-gun noses most often associated with B-26Ks were the norm for firepower.[17] (The YB-26K included six .50-caliber guns in the wings, a feature deleted on production K-models.) Production Counter Invaders also deleted the YB-26K's nosewheel steering, air conditioning, and JATO bottle racks.[18]

Armaments available for use on the eight underwing pylons included XM75 grenade launchers; P-2 grenade dispensers; rocket launch-

Figure 127. Pilots Cockpit Enclosure Installation

2-402

Invader cockpit glazing could include internal armor glass to provide frontal protection for the pilot (detail 'C').

ers including LAU-3A, MA3, Aero 6A, and LAU-10A, as well as the MA3 rocket adapter; SUU12 .50-caliber machine gun pod; and bombs ranging from 25 to 1,000 pounds, including 750-pound M117, 500-pound BLU-10/B, and BLU-10A/B fire bombs, and many others.

To ensure wing integrity, new skin was applied to the upper and lower surfaces of the wings between the spars; new forward and rear spar webs were installed, and steel straps were added to the spar caps.

The On Mark B-26K was fitted with improved R-2800 engines with water injection, producing 2,500 horsepower for takeoff, versus the previous 2,000 takeoff horsepower of the regular Invader's Dash-79 engines. Broad paddle Hamilton-Standard reversible pitch propellers fitted to B-26Ks enhanced shorter landing rolls, as did the use of powerful antiskid brakes.

The upgraded brakes were in fact part of a package of KC-135 brakes, wheels, and tires applied to the

Counter Invader.[19]

K-models were equipped with dual flight controls in the cockpit. They could be configured with an eight-gun nose or switched to a glass nose for reconnaissance. When the glass nose was in place, the second set of flight controls was removed to allow access to and from the nose. The requirement for dual controls was rooted in a rule of engagement at the time Counter Invaders were conceived, which said a South Vietnamese pilot had to be at the controls of an airplane actually in combat; this later gave way to overt American combat missions.

A pallet was devised to carry the F-492 reconnaissance camera system in the bomb bay of the B-26K, and Counter Invaders could be modified with camera windows in their bomb bay doors, covered by plates when not in use.

Responding to changes in handling brought about by all of the upgrades to the Counter Invader, B-26Ks were given rudders slightly broader in chord than traditional

A-26s had. This was apparent in the way the trailing edge of the new rudder met the rear end cap of the fuselage on the K-model.

In the last years of service before withdrawal by the Air Force in 1969, the B-26K was redesignated A-26A, a convenience that paid technical homage to host country Thailand, who at that time would not allow American bombers to be based there, but would permit attack aircraft. Some Counter Invaders were furnished as military aid to countries other than South Vietnam.

This ultimate iteration of the Invader line was potent enough to spark rivalry and contention between A-26 advocates and jet proponents in the Air Force in the late 1960s, certainly a tribute to the basic Invader design of the 1940s.

Invader Model Variants

It is a credit to the thoroughness of the Douglas A-26 design team that the basic airframe changed so little over its production run. Variations in military A-26s include:

B-26K (64-17666) used square-tipped paddle prop blades for performance improvements. Impressive clusters of ordnance were carried on eight pylons mounted to a beefed-up wing structure. (Bowers collection)

A-26B fitted with six-gun nose shows enormous length of engine nacelles, which gave rise to comments from NACA during early design studies of the Invader. (San Diego Aerospace Museum)

XA-26: The first Invader (41-19504), rolled out with the Plexiglas bombardier's nose.

XA-26A: Number two in the A-26 family (41-19505), fitted with four ventral 20-mm cannons and an elongated radar nose, as a potential nightfighter.

XA-26B: Third prototype Invader (41-19588), fitted with a 75-mm cannon in a solid nose.

A-26B: A major production variant with solid strafing nose configured for six, and later eight, .50-caliber machine guns. Douglas Long Beach built 1,150 A-26Bs, while the company's Tulsa, Oklahoma, facility made 205 B-models.

A-26C: The other main production Invader model, fitted with a transparent bombardier nose; some retained a pair of forward-firing .50-caliber guns on the right side of this nose. Five C-models were built at Long Beach; 1,086 at Tulsa in 1945.

XA-26D: Lone example (possibly converted from A-26B number 44-34776) made with eight-gun nose plus six more .50-calibers in wing packages, and incorporating powerplant improvements; end of World War Two prompted cancellation of order for 750 D-models, but armament upgrades survived to appear on some B-models.

A-26E: Canceled version that was to have improved upon the A-26C.

XA-26F: Actually an A-26B airframe (44-34586) used as a testbed for a General Electric J31 turbojet in the rear fuselage.

B-26J: Standardized nomenclature for U.S. Navy Invaders previously tagged JD-1, and used for utility purposes including target towing.

B-26K: Dramatically beefed-up Counter Invader developed by On Mark Engineering of Van Nuys, California, in 1963, using fixed wingtip gasoline tanks and new underwing hardpoints on a strengthened wing. Later redesignated A-26A when based by the U.S. Air Force in Thailand in the late 1960s.

RB-26L: Vietnam-era reconnaissance model; saw limited service using Reconofax IV infrared sensors and cameras originally intended for supersonic B-58s.

A-26Z: Douglas Aircraft's unbuilt postwar Invader proposal, featuring droppable gasoline tanks on the wingtips and crew entry through the nosewheel well, did not fulfill an Air Force need at the time.

[1] "Case History of A-26 Airplane," compiled by Historical Division, Intelligence, T-2, Air Technical Service Command, Wright Field, Oct 1945. [2] Ibid. [3] Ibid. [4] Ibid. [5] Ibid. [6] Ibid. [7] Ibid. [8] Ibid. [9] Memo, Gen. H.H. Arnold to Gen. Oliver P. Echols and Gen. Barney Giles, "Modification of Airplanes," 13 March 1944 (Air Force Historical Research Agency). [10] Memo, Maj. Gen. Oliver P. Echols to Gen. Barney Giles, "Modification of Airplanes," 16 March 1944 (Air Force Historical Research Agency). [11] "Case History of A-26 Airplane," compiled by Historical Division, Intelligence, T-2, Air Technical Service Command, Wright Field, Oct 1945. [12] Ibid. [13] Ibid. [14] Ibid. [15] Army Air Forces Statistical Digest — World War II, Office of Statistical Control, HQ AAF, December 1945. [16] "Case History of A-26 Airplane," compiled by Historical Division, Intelligence, T-2, Air Technical Service Command, Wright Field, Oct 1945. [17] "Fact Sheet — B-26K 'Counter Invader'," Furman Associates, Los Angeles, California, circa 1963. [18] "First B-26K Delivery Planned Next Month," Aviation Week and Space Technology, Pp. 96-97, 18 May 1964. [19] Ibid.

WORLD WAR TWO

The first A-26s to enter combat had the early flush canopies which greatly restricted lateral vision over the engine nacelles. Given bad reviews by Fifth Air Force in the Pacific following their July 1944 battle debut, A-26s were nonetheless, in November 1944, selected to replace all European A-20 groups and all but three European B-26 Marauder groups by the end of July 1945.[1]

Those first Fifth Air Force crews who took Invaders into combat in the summer of 1944 on tactical suitability evaluations came from the Third Bomb Group. The massive engine nacelles, at the same height as the pilot, came in for criticism because they precluded low-level loose line-abreast formation attacks, wherein the pilots needed to be able to see other aircraft in the vicinity. With underwing gun packages installed, the forward firepower was praised by the pilots, although the 25-mph speed penalty imposed by the wing gun packages was criticized. As noted in an AAF study: "Elevator forces required for low altitude pull-outs were considered too great, range was inadequate, the location of the life raft was unsatisfactory, and the bottom turret was thought to be unnecessary. The A-26 liaison officer made recommendations for changes to correct these deficiencies. Ground personnel found the A-26 airplanes satisfactory from the maintenance standpoint, except for certain difficulties encountered with the electrical system, air filters, and fuel selector valves."[2]

Douglas engineers in California pioneered a new raised canopy to give the pilot better visibility; later, their fellows in Oklahoma would adapt the raised canopies to Tulsa Invaders as well. When the commander of the Third Bomb Group had an opportunity to fly the prototype raised-canopy Invader in the fall of 1944, he pronounced the resulting aircraft suitable for Southwest Pacific operations.

By October 1944, Maj. Gen. Hoyt S. Vandenberg was relaying results of Ninth Air Force's combat debut with A-26s in Europe. Ninth Air Force's first A-26 sorties did not amount to a complete and conclusive test due to a coincidence in the time of their arrival, because at that time, according to an AAF paper, "the principal difficulty was lack of targets for testing the airplane at low altitudes and making maximum use of forward firepower." Nonetheless, the Invader's combat debut in Ninth Air Force convinced General Vandenberg that the A-26 was a suitable replacement for Martin B-26s and Douglas A-20s in the Ninth Bombardment Division.[3]

Summarizing the Ninth Air Force experience with 18 A-26s sent to the United Kingdom in the summer of 1944, and used on eight combat missions, the AAF said: "It was concluded that the A-26 was a very effective medium bomber with a larger load than the A-20 airplane, greater range than either the A-20 or (Martin) B-26 airplane, and with superior single engine performance. Its speed advantage, flying characteristics, maneuverability, and ease of maintaining formation permitted longer missions with less crew fatigue. On the missions flown, gasoline consumption was lower and radius of action was greater than had been expected."

A-26B-60-DL (44-34486) paused at Barrackpore, Calcutta, India, on 20 September 1945 for a portrait by aviation enthusiast and AAF officer Peter M. Bowers. Pylon for drop tank is visible. (Peter M. Bowers)

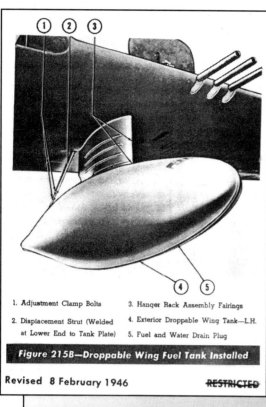

A-26 drop tank pylon could carry a stamped steel 165-gallon gas tank, but crews were told to limit its capacity to only 155 gallons because of the angle at which the tank was suspended. A displacement strut (item 2 in artwork from a maintenance manual), welded to the tank and resting in a socket in the underside of the wing, precluded the empty drop tank from striking the A-26 as it departed when jettisoned.

Invader based on how it would be fielded. All European A-20 groups and all but three Martin B-26 groups were slated for conversion to A-26s by the end of July 1945, comprising 11 A-26 groups. At this time, FEAF continued to eschew A-26s, but there were those in the AAF who "believed that the extreme prejudice of the FEAF against A-26 airplanes was not justified when it was considered that the four A-26B airplanes furnished them for operational tests were four of the first production airplanes and incorporated a number of undesirable features," according to the AAF A-26 case study. Those deliberating A-26

The Invader could also carry drop tanks modified for use as napalm bombs. Possibly because they were dropped when full, the napalm tanks did not require a displacement strut to avoid striking the A-26. (Bowers collection)

A Ninth Bomb Division report, summarized in the AAF A-26 case history, described early A-26 combat formations as presenting "no great difficulties after pilots became accustomed to the limited visibility caused by the high nacelles," no doubt referring to early flush-canopy variants of the Invader.[4]

If tooling and production hurdles bedeviled the A-26 early in its career, it is nonetheless a tribute to the thoroughness of the Douglas design team that the Invader received such high praise on its introduction in Europe. The canopy modification was to be the most pronounced visible change to the Invader; it was basically a sound bomber early on.

The AAF in November 1944 formulated production plans for the procurement and deployment in the AAF wanted to replace B-25s in other theaters with A-26s as soon as the Invaders were available. Recommended order for conversion to A-26s was: 1. European Theater of Operations; 2. Mediterranean Theater of Operations; 3. China-Burma-India Theater of Operations; 4. AAF-POA; 5. Far East Air Forces; 6. North Pacific.[5] (In execution, some changes in order occurred.)

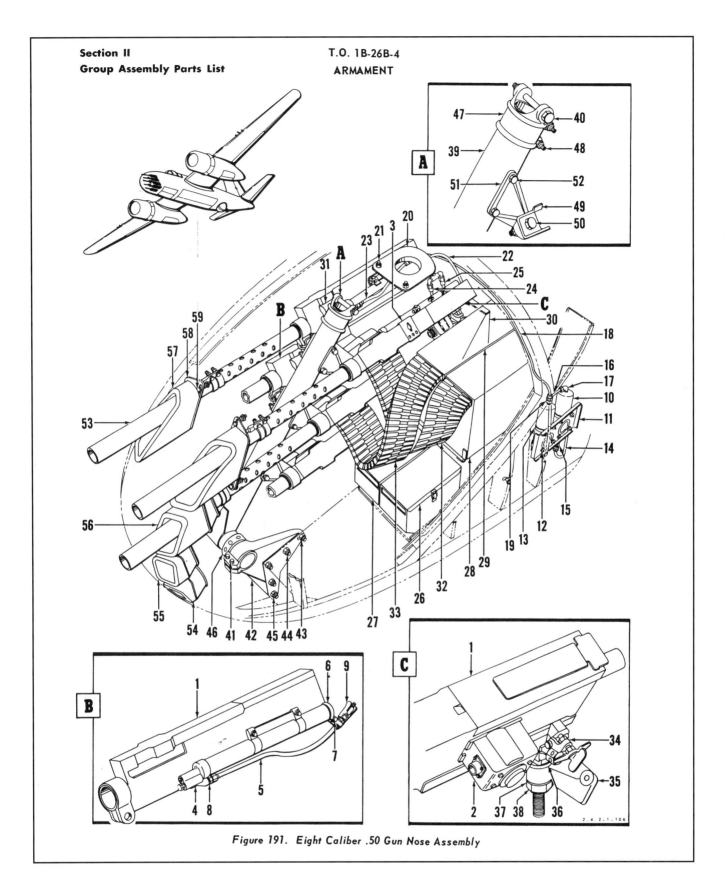

Figure 191. Eight Caliber .50 Gun Nose Assembly

A-26 eight-gun nose for .50-caliber M-2 machine guns contained support structure (detail 'A' in drawing) and ammo boxes (numbers 26 through 29). Guns were canted to facilitate operability, and staggered fore and aft to allow for ammunition feedways. In detail 'B,' the long tube (items 4 and 5) make up a pneumatic gun charger.

C-18463-1   A-26 B   10-9-44

Raised cockpit canopy on A-26B-20-DL gave pilot additional visibility to the sides, over the large engine nacelles. With adoption of raised canopy, two overhead hatches hinged outward instead of the forward-hinging overhead hatch of the first A-26s. (Douglas/Harry Gann)

Who's Who in WW2

In the Pacific, Seventh Air Force's 319th Bomb Group took on A-26s in the summer of 1945. Ninth Air Force's European Invaders equipped the 386th, 391st, 409th, 410th, and 416th Bomb Groups. In Tenth Air Force, the battle-hardened 12th Bomb Group began swapping its beloved B-25s for A-26s in the late summer of 1945, but did not use Invaders against the Japanese. Twelfth Air Force's 47th Bomb Group received some A-26s late in the European war.

Learning the A-26

The new Invader pilot had a remarkable warplane in his hands. In level flight, there were no top airspeed limitations; in a dive at a weight of 29,500 pounds or less, the twin-engine bomber could permissibly hit 425 miles an hour. On A-26s equipped with spoilers for improving airflow around the bomb bay, the bay doors could be opened all the way up to that top diving speed. Though fast and maneuverable, the A-26 was nonetheless restricted from being

flown in loops, intentional spins, inverted flight, and rolls. Supplemental fuel tanks, including droppable underwing 155-gallon teardrop tanks, could extend the Invader's range.[6]

Cruising speed for the A-26B and C-production models was 284 miles an hour; the gun-nose B-model had a top level speed of 355 miles an hour; the glass-nose A-26C could hit 373 miles an hour in level flight.[7]

Crew complement for a gun-nose A-26B consisted of "a pilot-radio

WARBIRD**TECH**
SERIES

Periscopic gunsight column in A-26 protruded above and below fuselage contours to afford gunner a sight picture for both remote power turrets. Item 36 in drawing from an A-26 illustrated parts book is the gunner's seat; item 49 is a seat belt.

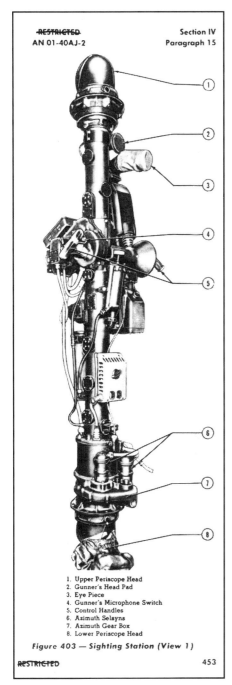

AN 01-40AJ-2

Section IV
Paragraph 15

1. Upper Periscope Head
2. Gunner's Head Pad
3. Eye Piece
4. Gunner's Microphone Switch
5. Control Handles
6. Azimuth Selsyns
7. Azimuth Gear Box
8. Lower Periscope Head

Figure 403 — Sighting Station (View 1)

453

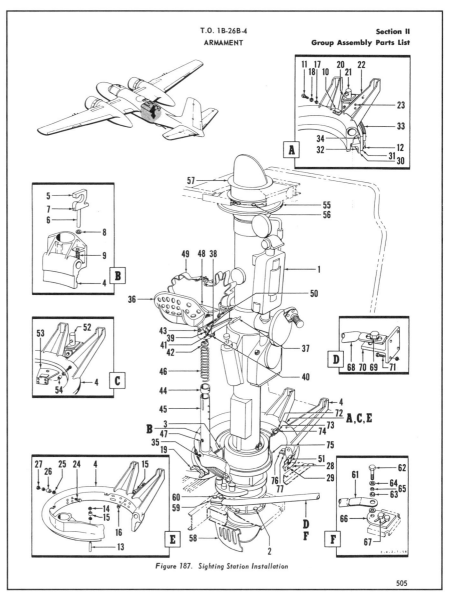

T.O. 1B-26B-4
ARMAMENT

Section II
Group Assembly Parts List

Figure 187. Sighting Station Installation

505

Artwork from an Invader erection and maintenance manual shows gunsight periscopic column. As the gunner moved the sight by means of hand grips, a prism was automatically deflected to allow viewing from the appropriate periscope, either upper or lower, as dictated by the movement initiated by the gunner. If the external periscope windows became iced or obscured by dirt, isopropyl alcohol fluid could be hand-pumped over the periscope windows, with the slipstream removing the ice or dirt accumulation after the alcohol loosened it.

operator, and a gun loader-navigator stationed in the pilot's compartment ... and a gunner located in an enclosed compartment ... aft of the bomb bay," according to an Invader "Dash-1" flight handbook. With the discontinuation of heavy cannons for Invaders, the gun-loading aspects of the navigator's chores diminished. The manual also noted: "The crew of the (glass-nosed) A-26C airplane is the same except that the gun loader-navigator is replaced by a bombardier-navigator. The bombardier normally rides on the bicycle type seat to the right of the pilot and moves to the bombardier's compartment for the actual bombing run."[8]

Some A-26s were fitted with dual controls; the copilot's control wheel was detachable to allow movement into the bombardier nose on A-26Cs. In flight, crew members could traverse the bomb bay to enter the forward or aft compartments, "provided a long range fuel tank, a smoke tank, torpedoes, or 500 or 1000 pound bombs are not being carried," the flight handbook explained. [9]

Takeoff

The new Invader pilot was instructed to set engine mixture controls to Auto Rich and supercharger blower controls to Low, ensure bomb bay doors were closed, and cowl flaps one-half open, and set takeoff flaps at 20 percent (recommended) or 15 percent (minimum). The pilot's actions with the A-26 on the ground were of concern; care had to be exercised to avoid nose-wheel structure damage, which initially plagued Invader operations. Notes in the flight handbook included a caution: "Both engines must be run up simultaneously in order to avoid damage to the nose wheel strut." During the takeoff roll, A-26 pilots were instructed: "When the stalling speed, for the weight and wing flap setting used, is reached, raise the nose wheel just clear of the ground. At this angle of attack, allow the airplane to fly clear of the ground." And for rough-field takeoffs, A-26 pilots were advised by the manual: "If the terrain is rough, it may be necessary to raise the nose wheel just off the ground before flying speed has been reached to avoid undue stress on the nose wheel structure." [10]

It was possible to reach flying speed before reaching minimum single-engine airspeed (single-engine airspeed was 140 miles an hour for takeoffs below weights of 32,000 pounds; 160 miles an hour for heavier takeoffs). If one engine failed in the air below single-engine airspeed, the pilot was

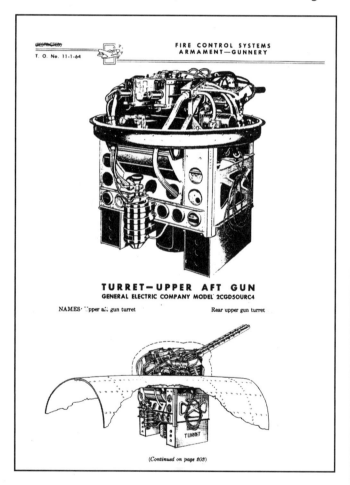

General Electric remote top turret, as depicted in a World War Two armaments manual, was smaller than a manned turret would need to be, saving space and affording better streamlining. (Bill Miranda collection)

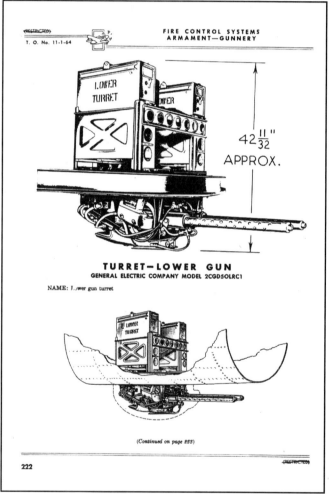

A-26 lower turret in many ways mirrored top turret by General Electric. (Bill Miranda collection)

instructed to close the throttles, lower wing flaps, and proceed straight ahead in preparation of landing. "If there are obstacles or rough terrain ahead, retract the landing gear," the handbook noted. Ignition, generator, and battery switches were to be placed in

Some A-26s were designed to carry a 75-mm cannon plus two .50-caliber machine guns in the nose. Gunner in aft compartment was sandwiched between the upper and lower turrets he commanded.

KEY TO FIGURE 534

1. Wing Gun Ammunition Boxes
2. Fire Control Panel
3. Gun Sight Rheostat
4. 75mm Cannon Shell Case Catcher
5. Upper Turret Ammunition Boxes
6. Upper Turret
7. Type M-2 Caliber .50 Turret Guns
8. Turret Control Box
9. Upper Periscope Head
10. Sighting Station
11. Lower Turret Ammunition Boxes
12. Lower Turret
13. Type M-2 Caliber .50 Turret Guns
14. Gunner's Seat
15. Turret Ammunition Box Hoisting Cable
16. Lower Periscope Head
17. Type M-2 Caliber .50 Wing Guns
18. Gun Charger Cable
19. Gun Charger Cable Handle
20. 75mm Shell Stowage Rack
21. Ring and Bead Sight
22. Cannon Firing Actuator Mechanism
23. Tell-Tale Indicator
24. T-13E1 75mm Cannon
25. Gun Sight Aiming Point Camera *
26. Nose Gun Ammunition Box
27. Type M-2 Caliber .50 Nose Guns
28. Cannon Feed and Ejection Chute
29. Type N-9 Gun Sight
30. Gun Firing Triggers (Guns and Cannon)

* Located in the Pilot's Compartment on some airplanes.

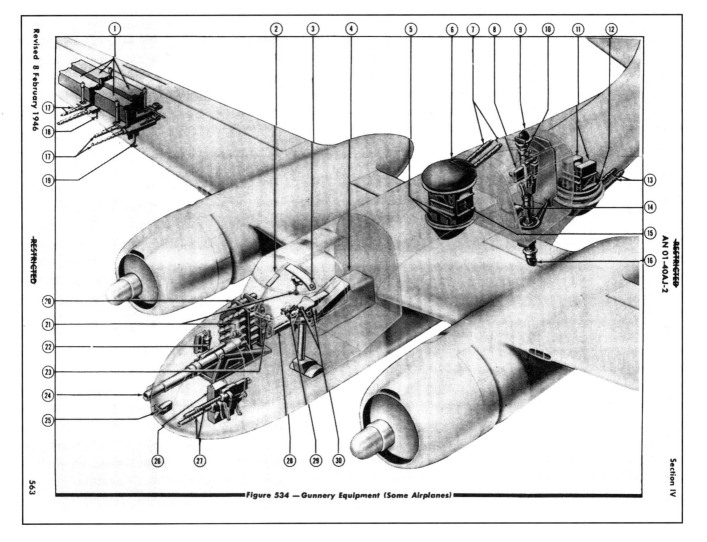

Figure 534 — Gunnery Equipment (Some Airplanes)

Revised 8 February 1946

RESTRICTED

RESTRICTED AN 01-40AJ-2

Section IV

563

the Off position; fuel tank selector valve control and fuel cross-feed and bomb bay tank selector valve control were to be in the Off position. In specific A-26s fitted with the engine oil and hydraulic fluid fire shut-off valves, these were to be closed.[11] Landing was to be straight ahead to preclude the possibility of a dangerous low-speed, low-altitude turn/stall mishap.

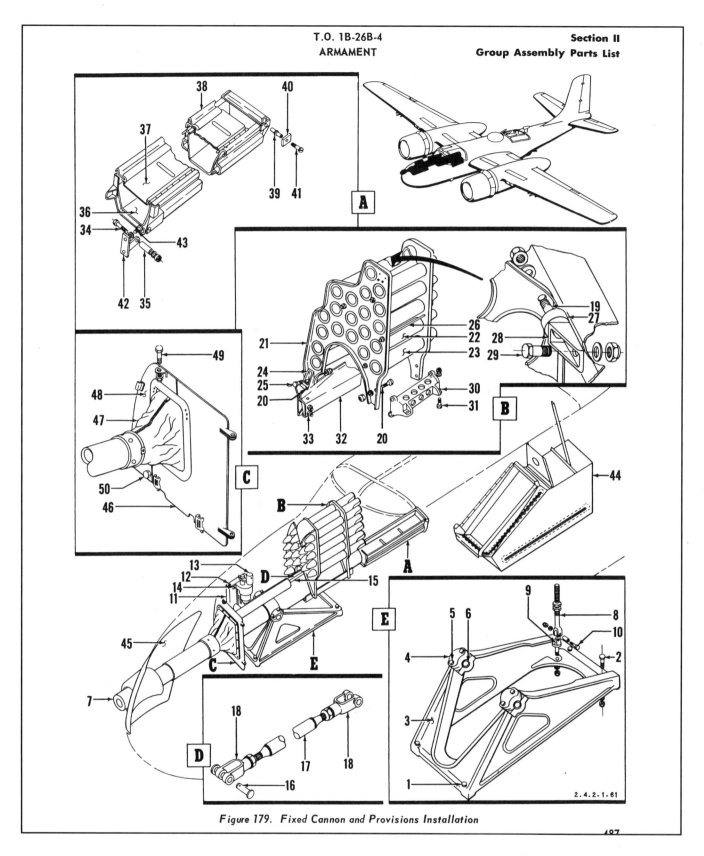

Figure 179. Fixed Cannon and Provisions Installation

2.4.2-1-61

The short-lived 75-mm cannon nose had racks for carrying 20 heavy rounds of ammunition (part numbers 21-33 in detail 'B' of the drawing). A seal (part number 47 in detail C) kept wind blast, and presumably gun gases, out of the aircraft. The 75-mm gun was installed at the time of delivery in A-26s numbers 41-39100 through 41-39119 and 43-22252 through 43-22266.

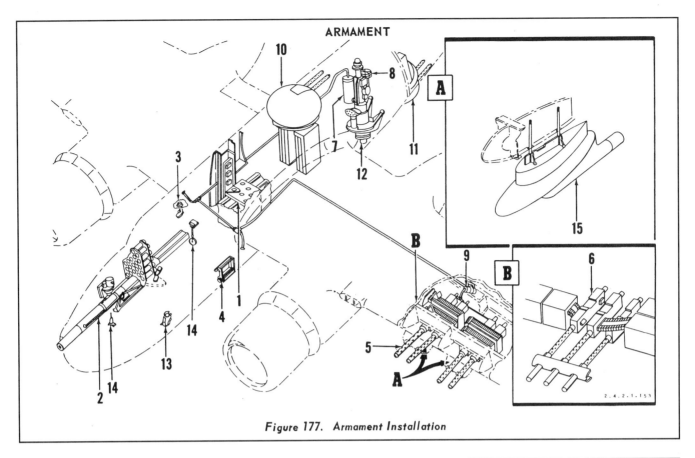

Figure 177. Armament Installation

A-26 wing gun installations could be three internal guns per wing or up to four pod-mounted .50-calibers under each wing. A smoke generator chemical tank (part number 15 in detail 'A' of the drawing) could be mounted beneath the wing. Part number 3 is a pyrotechnic installation allowing a flare gun to be used for signaling purposes.

Handling Qualities

The broad, flat bomb bay doors of the Invader had an effect on stability when open in flight. The flight manual noted: "No longitudinal change, but the airplane becomes very stable directionally." Center of gravity loads for the A-26 were limited at 18 to 32 percent MAC (mean aerodynamic chord). At the extremes of center-of-gravity loadings for the Invader, "instability is approached," the manual noted almost laconically.[12]

Although not intended for true dive bombing, the A-26 could be dived (depending on weight) to a speed of 425 miles per hour. The handbook explained: "If trimmed 'hands off' in level flight at cruising power there will be no appreciable change in trim during the dive. Do not use trim tabs to aid in recovering from dives, as excessive load factors may be encountered." Cowl flaps were to be closed in dives. Rapid pull-outs were to be avoided.[13]

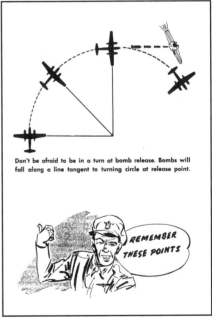

Don't be afraid to be in a turn at bomb release. Bombs will fall along a line tangent to turning circle at release point.

REMEMBER THESE POINTS

World War Two AAF Bombardier's Information File used A-26 silhouettes to depict bomb release in a turn, with the bombs following a straight path upon release.

[1] "Case History of A-26 Airplane," compiled by Historical Division, Intelligence, T-2, Air Technical Service Command, Wright Field, Oct 1945. [2] Ibid. [3] Ibid. [4] Ibid. [5] Ibid. [6] Handbook Flight Operating Instructions — USAF Series B-26B, B-26C; Navy Model JD-1 Aircraft, 10 August 1945, Revised 21 November 1950. [7] Peter M. Bowers and Gordon Swanborough, United States Military Aircraft Since 1908, Putnam, London, 1971. [8] Handbook Flight Operating Instructions — USAF Series B-26B, B-26C; Navy Model JD-1 Aircraft, 10 August 1945, Revised 21 November 1950. [9] Ibid. [10] Ibid. [11] Ibid. [12] Ibid. [13] Ibid.

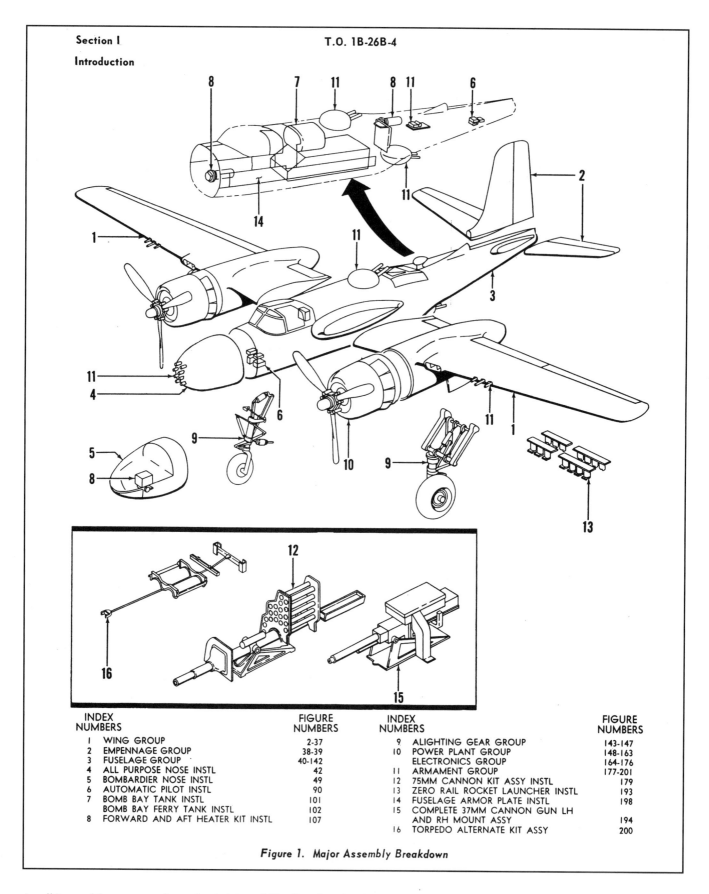

INDEX NUMBERS		FIGURE NUMBERS	INDEX NUMBERS		FIGURE NUMBERS
1	WING GROUP	2-37	9	ALIGHTING GEAR GROUP	143-147
2	EMPENNAGE GROUP	38-39	10	POWER PLANT GROUP	148-163
3	FUSELAGE GROUP	40-142		ELECTRONICS GROUP	164-176
4	ALL PURPOSE NOSE INSTL	42	11	ARMAMENT GROUP	177-201
5	BOMBARDIER NOSE INSTL	49	12	75MM CANNON KIT ASSY INSTL	179
6	AUTOMATIC PILOT INSTL	90	13	ZERO RAIL ROCKET LAUNCHER INSTL	193
7	BOMB BAY TANK INSTL	101	14	FUSELAGE ARMOR PLATE INSTL	198
	BOMB BAY FERRY TANK INSTL	102	15	COMPLETE 37MM CANNON GUN LH	
8	FORWARD AND AFT HEATER KIT INSTL	107		AND RH MOUNT ASSY	194
			16	TORPEDO ALTERNATE KIT ASSY	200

Figure 1. Major Assembly Breakdown

In all its multi-purpose glory, the A-26 could be fitted with a 37-mm cannon (part number 15), although in common practice, operational gun-nosed Invaders carried six or eight .50-caliber machine guns.

During training in Florence, South Carolina, Invader number 41-39420 came to rest on its chin. View shows how the large-diameter nosewheel stowed flat in the fuselage. Slot in fuselage just aft of nosewheel well allowed baffles to extend, curbing turbulent air from entering the open bomb bay. (AFHRA)

Bane of early A-26 operations, nosegear problems led to two bent props on a B-model at Florence Army Airfield, South Carolina, on 12 July 1945. (U.S. Air Force)

Collapsed left main gear hobbled Invader number 43-22438, an early B-model, during training at Florence, South Carolina on 11 June 1945. (U.S. Air Force)

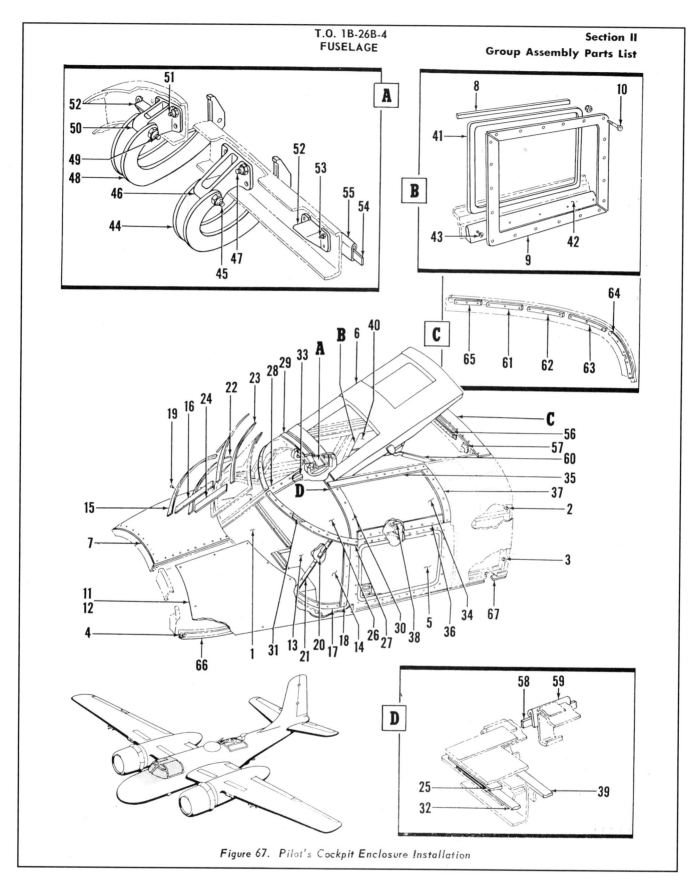

Figure 67. Pilot's Cockpit Enclosure Installation

Early right-side forward hinging cockpit hatch; this was replaced when A-26 canopy height was raised during production to afford better visibility to the side.

KOREA AND THE COLD WAR

SOMETHING OLD, SOMETHING NEW

B-26 Invaders flew all manner of day and night sorties against fixed and mobile targets during the Korean war. Some criticism was leveled against the Invader by planners in the Air Force who said the B-26 was ill-suited to coping with the mountainous terrain of Korea, especially on night missions. This begs the question: What aircraft of the era could have done any better? Airmen crewing B-26s faced death, and performed admirably. Ironically, that same Invader was the bomber at hand a decade later when counter-insurgency warplanes were required for the expanding conflict in Vietnam (sometimes over a less upthrust battlefield).

First offensive air action of the Korean war by Far East Air Forces (FEAF) was a 28 June 1950 strike by a dozen B-26s over marshaling yards in South Korea. This strike came three days after North Korea invaded the south. FEAF's initial Invader complement was 26 B-26s under Fifth Air Force. Initially based in Japan, the Invaders' commuting distance to the battle front robbed B-26 crews of spontaneity in target selection, thereby limiting their ability to capitalize on rapid enemy developments. Invaders were thrust into night intruder operations partly out of exasperation with limits

The postwar period saw B-26s migrate to Air National Guard units, as utility aircraft as well as bombers. This B-model (44-34672), minus nose armament, carried the dagger-punctured ace-of-spades emblem of Washington's 116th Fighter Squadron when photographed at Felts Field in Spokane on 3 April 1949. (Don Keller collection)

Bold abbreviation "WN NG" for Washington National Guard, bracketed insignia on the fuselage of the 116th Fighter Squadron's Invader. (Don Keller collection)

In December 1946, this black A-26C-10-DL carried a ventral radome—and a recruiting message urging: "Join the Regular Army." (Gordon S. Williams via Peter M. Bowers)

placed on other aircraft at that time in 1950—the few radar-equipped F-82 Twin Mustangs initially were kept for the air defense of Japan; F-80s were too fast for typical nocturnal target acquisition; and machine gun muzzle blasts from F-51 Mustangs degraded the pilot's night vision. The only other option was the B-26; if the Air Force's ability to wage war at night was limited in 1950, fault hardly lies with the B-26 or its crews. Into 1951, quantity was a problem for FEAF; typically only about 120-140 Invaders were available to Fifth Air Force, and only about 75 B-26s could be ready for missions on any given day.[1]

Black Tulsa-built C-model, possibly from 47th Bomb Group, used radome; fixed nose gun ports have been faired over. Photo probably was made on orthographic film, rendering insignia blue relatively light, and small tail numbers (435966) dark, indicating they probably were painted red. (H.L. Martin/Warren Bodie)

Its bomb bay shortened to accommodate radar, a black B-26 uses wing shackles to bomb up for a mission over Korea.

An airman checks the top General Electric turret of his B-26 used over Korea. Diameter, height, and spread of the guns was smaller on unmanned Invader, Superfortress, and Black Widow turrets that on older manned turrets.

When North Korean convoys began plying the roads at night in July 1950, the drivers initially naively kept their vehicles' headlights switched on, giving the B-26 crews beacons to bomb. After several setbacks in which Invaders rampaged among illuminated trucks, the communist drivers learned to do without flagrantly visible lights. This forced the B-26s to team up with flare-droppers to highlight the enemy trucks. By the summer of 1951, FEAF B-26s were playing a part in the Korean war's own Operation Strangle, striving to cut transport lines, as had the similarly named operation in Italy during World War Two. One trick assigned to the Invaders was spreading cluster bombs around cratered roads, to make repair more treacherous, and hopefully, time-consuming by littering the ground with anti-personnel bomblets that would explode on contact. [2]

By June of 1951, another B-26 squadron was dispatched to aid the United Nations effort in Korea, with communist night truck convoys still a thorny problem. In mountainous regions of Korea, night-flying Invaders sometimes had to attack from a mile above the ground to stay clear of obstacles; in the more gentle terrain to the west, attack altitudes of 1,500 feet still were considered by some in Fifth Air Force to be higher than desirable for effective gunnery. During heightened attacks on rail lines in 1951, the increased volume of traffic on roads as a result made for many Invader opportunities. By

An Invader gunner shows his work station for a publicity photo in Korea. Elevating or depressing the grips would automatically transfer the periscopic view from upper to lower hemispheres if both turrets were fitted.

Armorers load .50-caliber ammunition belts in a six-gun nose of an Invader bound for a sortie over Korea. Smooth blast tubes covered barrels of guns in this installation.

Silver B-26 with broad red propeller arc warning band ahead of 40 bomb mission symbols gets bombed up for another sortie over Korea. (Douglas/Harry Gann)

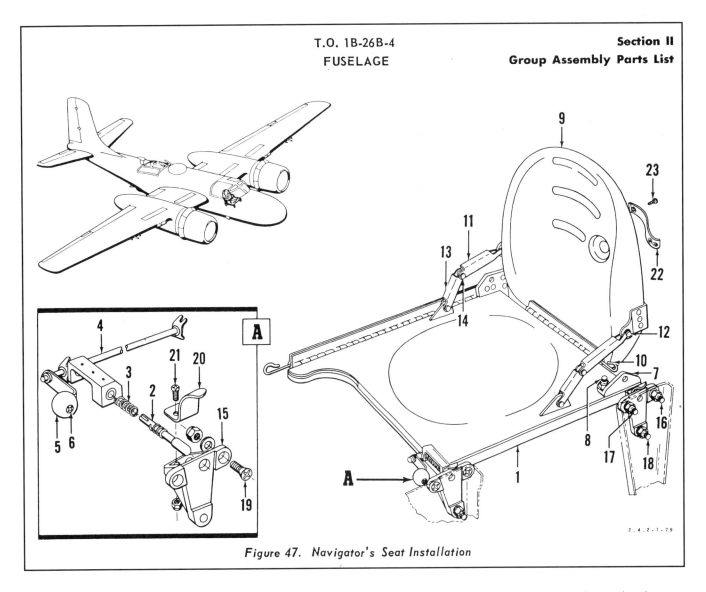

2.4.2.1-79

Figure 47. Navigator's Seat Installation

A seat was provided for a navigator on the right side of the A-26 cockpit, as shown in an illustrated parts book.

that time, one wing of Invaders prowled out of Kunsan, another from Pusan, in South Korea, rather than distant Japan. As replacement B-26s came to Korea, an increasing number of glass-nosed bombers entered the ranks. With fewer guns, and provision for a bombardier, these Invaders placed emphasis on bombing enemy transport instead of strafing it. Soon, B-26 crew claims for trucks destroyed were rising dramatically. For one August night alone, B-26 crews claimed to have damaged or destroyed almost 800 vehicles. It was difficult, in the cloaking darkness, to determine accurate damage assessments, and daytime reconnaissance was in too much demand to be used for after-the-fact truck counting.[3]

When Maj. Gen. Glenn O. Barcus assumed command of Fifth Air Force in 1952, he questioned the glowing claims of trucks decimated by nocturnal Invaders. General Barcus orchestrated a test, for which hand-picked B-26 crews from the two night interdiction wings were told to bomb and strafe, in daylight, trucks placed on a target range. Test results were sobering: Only five percent of the bombs hit within 75 feet of the aiming point, and trucks not carrying volatile cargoes were not likely to be damaged by bombs falling more than 50 feet away. Gunnery accuracy in the tests, from a range of 2,000 feet, produced about two percent hits on a target 10 feet by 10 feet.[4] Yet the B-26 crews can not be dismissed lightly; to be sure, they accounted for the demolition of a portion of the enemy's transportation, and they clearly forced convoys into defensive modes of operation less efficient than simple, lighted, over-the-road driving.

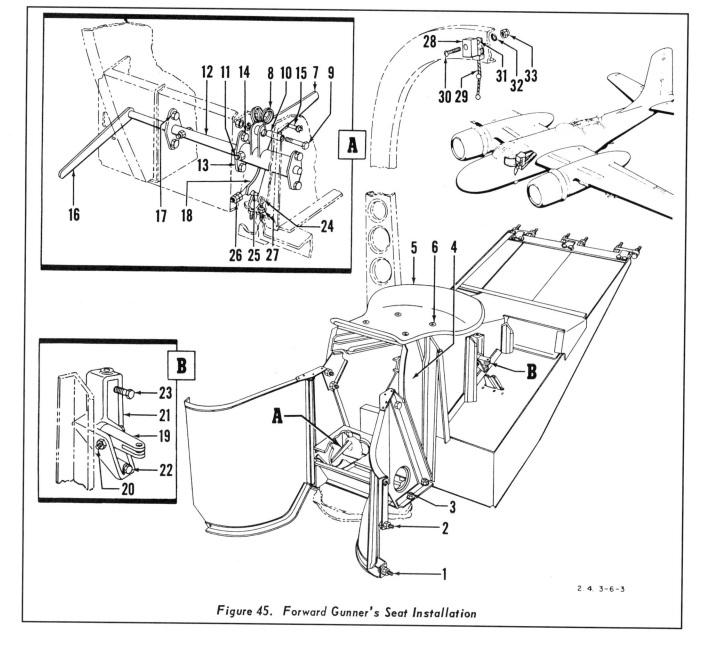

Figure 45. Forward Gunner's Seat Installation

Forward gunner's seat (part number 5) in the A-26 was a metal tractor-type saddle.

In addition to transport-busting, B-26s in Korea, beginning about May 1951, sometimes teamed with air and ground reconnaissance and MPQ-2 portable radar sets to designate close-air support targets for the Invader crews. At times during the war, Eighth Army and Fifth Air Force teamed to use radar to guide Invaders over Chinese troop concentrations with success.[5]

Among the black Invaders hunting transportation targets in Korea by night were other more clandestine B-26s. By the first half of 1952, B Flight of the 6167th Operations Squadron had glass-nosed Invaders stationed at K-16 airfield in Seoul. Modified with wooden bench seating in the bomb bay, these unarmed B-26s could carry as many as six parachutists behind enemy lines, sometimes as far as Manchuria.[6]

[1] Eduard Mark, *Aerial Interdiction in Three Wars,* Center for Air Force History, Washington, D.C., 1994, and Benjamin Franklin Cooling, Editor, *Case Studies in the Development of Close Air Support,* Office of Air Force History, Washington, D.C., 1990. [2] Eduard Mark, *Aerial Interdiction in Three Wars,* Center for Air Force History, Washington, D.C., 1994. [3] *Ibid.* [4] *Ibid.* [5] Benjamin Franklin Cooling, Editor, *Case Studies in the Development of Close Air Support,* Office of Air Force History, Washington, D.C., 1990. [6] Col. Michael E. Haas, USAF (Ret), *Apollo's Warriors — United States Air Force Special Operations during the Cold War,* Air University Press, Maxwell AFB, Alabama, 1997.

Interchangeable noses make it difficult to assume Invader models by their appearance. This is a B-26C with a solid gun nose, circa 1956. The style of tail numbering on this aircraft (0-435267) was applied to Air Force aircraft more than 10 years old beginning in the 1950s; the prefix "0" is the clue. As the Air Force fleet aged, and many aircraft long outlived a decade of service, this practice was discontinued. (Don Keller collection)

Staged ordnance photo during Korean War shows 100-pound bombs, four scuffed napalm tanks, and around 6,000 rounds of .50-caliber ammunition. Pilot Lt. Col. Joseph Belser, left, and Sgt. Alfred Head, crew chief, both from the 3rd Bomb Group, posed for the photo. (Bowers collection)

Location of engine exhaust ports is manifest by smudges on this silver A-26B-DT (43-22305). Old style canopy required a brace to hold it open. (Don Keller collection)

U.S. Air Force B-26 drone carrier was photographed with a target under both wings. Red propeller warning band extended onto opened nosewheel doors. (Warren Bodie via Peter M. Bowers)

PASSPORT TO POSTERITY

Never a candidate for wartime Lend Lease, the A-26 remained primarily a USAF bomber until postwar efforts made Invaders available to American allies. The patchwork of A-26s in varied government uses in the decades after World War Two added to the fabric of the Cold War.

Invaders Abroad

A-26s formed a significant part of the air forces of many countries around the globe, in some cases more than two decades after the end of World War Two. (A detailed treatment of A-26s in international military use is found in *Foreign Invaders—The Douglas Invader in Foreign Military and U.S. Clandestine Service* by Dan Hagedorn and Leif Hellstrom, published originally by Midland Publishing Limited in the UK in 1994, and distributed in North America by Specialty Press.)

Foreign military users of Douglas A/B-26 Invaders included: Biafra, Brazil, Chile, Colombia, Cuba, Dominican Republic, El Salvador, France, Great Britain, Guatemala, Honduras, Indonesia, Mexico, Nicaragua, Peru, Portugal, Saudi Arabia, South Vietnam, and Turkey.[1]

Masquerade over Cuba Turned Deadly

In one of the strangest of Cold War operations in which Douglas Invaders were involved, both sides in the combat had B-26s. Circa 1960, U.S. agents began laying plans, called Operation Pluto, for a paramilitary action against Fidel Castro's Cuba. Fifteen B-26s were obtained from surplus at Davis-Monthan Air Force Base, Tucson, Arizona, and repainted in the markings of Castro's Cuban air force. Air National Guardsmen from Alabama, only recently turning in their B-26s, were recruited to help train Cuban expatriate pilots who were expected to fly the B-26s in support of an invasion by other expatriates at Cuba's Bay of Pigs in 1961.[2]

The operation included a ruse—one of the counterfeit Cuban B-26s was flown to Miami, Florida, on 15 April 1961, the day the other B-26s were attacking a Cuban airfield near the Bay of Pigs. The arrival of one of the Invaders in

Built as a glass-nosed A-26C-30-DT (44-35230), this black Invader in French service subsequently was fitted with a solid nose. France used Invaders in Indochina up to 1954, and later that decade over Algeria. This example was in French service circa late 1956-59. (E.M. Sommerich via Peter M. Bowers)

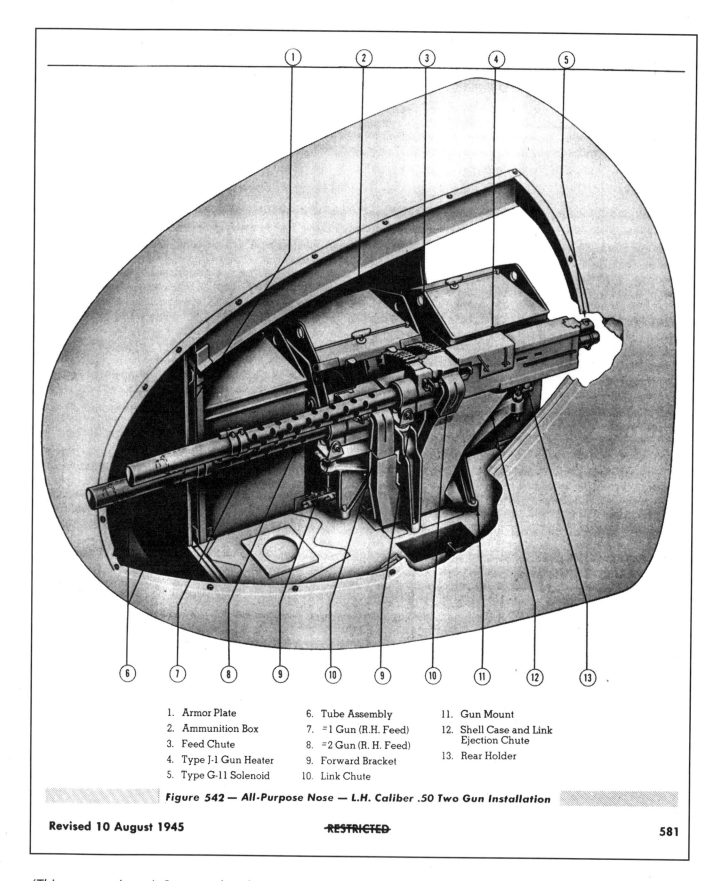

1. Armor Plate
2. Ammunition Box
3. Feed Chute
4. Type J-1 Gun Heater
5. Type G-11 Solenoid
6. Tube Assembly
7. ≠1 Gun (R.H. Feed)
8. ≠2 Gun (R. H. Feed)
9. Forward Bracket
10. Link Chute
11. Gun Mount
12. Shell Case and Link Ejection Chute
13. Rear Holder

Figure 542 — All-Purpose Nose — L.H. Caliber .50 Two Gun Installation

(This page and next): Staggered and asymmetrical six-gun array was used in the all-purpose nose. Flat armor plate inside the front of the nose provided frontal protection for the pilot as well as aircraft vital components farther aft.

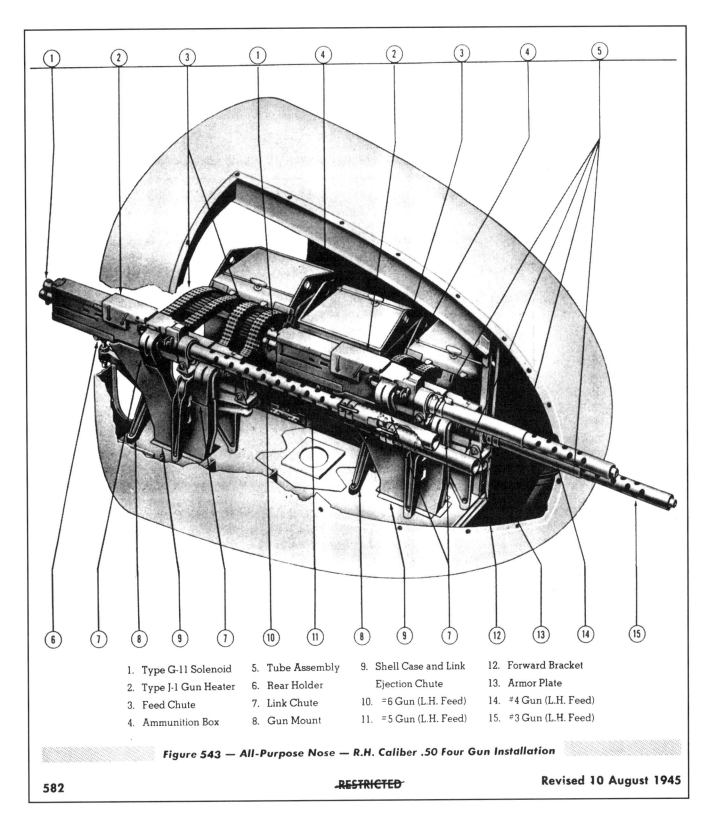

1. Type G-11 Solenoid
2. Type J-1 Gun Heater
3. Feed Chute
4. Ammunition Box
5. Tube Assembly
6. Rear Holder
7. Link Chute
8. Gun Mount
9. Shell Case and Link Ejection Chute
10. ⹀6 Gun (L.H. Feed)
11. ⹀5 Gun (L.H. Feed)
12. Forward Bracket
13. Armor Plate
14. #4 Gun (L.H. Feed)
15. #3 Gun (L.H. Feed)

Figure 543 — All-Purpose Nose — R.H. Caliber .50 Four Gun Installation

RESTRICTED **Revised 10 August 1945**

Miami was called a defection, amid protests from Cuba and studied indignation from American officials. But the "defecting" B-26, and others shot down over Cuba, were gun-nose variants; Castro's air force had glass-nose Invaders, and this discrepancy, and evident subterfuge, became public knowledge. When initial air strikes did not take out all of Castro's meager fighter force of a scant few armed T-33 jets and piston-engine Hawker Sea Furies, the next authorized mission for the Invaders saw 10 B-26s return over Cuba on 17 April, where the T-33s claimed at least four B-26s shot down; a fifth Invad-

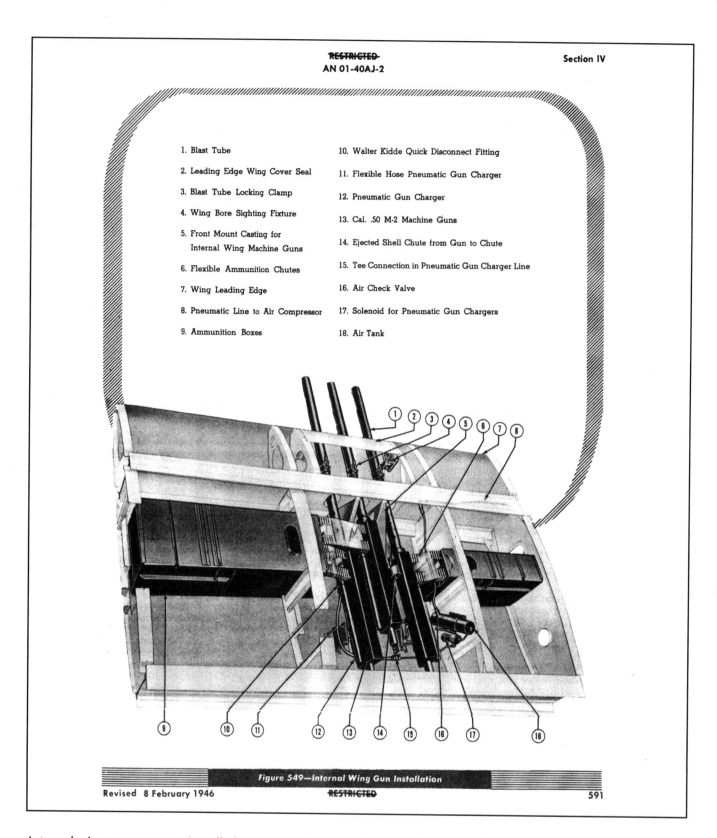

1. Blast Tube

2. Leading Edge Wing Cover Seal

3. Blast Tube Locking Clamp

4. Wing Bore Sighting Fixture

5. Front Mount Casting for
   Internal Wing Machine Guns

6. Flexible Ammunition Chutes

7. Wing Leading Edge

8. Pneumatic Line to Air Compressor

9. Ammunition Boxes

10. Walter Kidde Quick Disconnect Fitting

11. Flexible Hose Pneumatic Gun Charger

12. Pneumatic Gun Charger

13. Cal. .50 M-2 Machine Guns

14. Ejected Shell Chute from Gun to Chute

15. Tee Connection in Pneumatic Gun Charger Line

16. Air Check Valve

17. Solenoid for Pneumatic Gun Chargers

18. Air Tank

Figure 549—Internal Wing Gun Installation

Revised 8 February 1946   591

Internal wing guns were re-installed on some Salvadoran Invaders. The original Douglas system, as depicted in an erection and maintenance manual view, included an air tank and pneumatic gun chargers. The air reservoir could be recharged by an air compressor on the right side of the rear gunner compartment, which serviced air tanks for all fixed guns in the Invader as needed. By staggering the center gun, and using a combination of right- and left-hand feeds, the three M-2 .50-caliber machine guns in each wing could be fed by one double-wide and one single-wide ammunition box, as depicted here, although technical orders mention the use of three boxes in each wing.

er also was lost that day. The following day, according to a published account of the failed invasion, six B-26s returned to bomb Cuba. On this date, two of the six bombers over Cuba were flown by Americans. Next day, two of five B-26s over the Bay of Pigs beachhead were downed; they both carried volunteer American crews, some of whom died in a shootout with Cubans after crash-landing nearby. The hoped-for uprising of disaffected Cubans against Castro did not materialize with the establishment of a beachhead at the Bay of Pigs, and the episode went down as a bitter event in America's Cold War chronology.[3]

Smudgy Invader (41-39472; U.S. registration N86482) may have been sprayed with oil to prevent corrosion. This Long Beach-built B-model wound up in El Salvador by August 1969, too late for combat in that country's brief war with neighboring Honduras. It was removed from the Salvadoran air force's roster by April 1974. (Esposito/Bowers)

[1] Dan Hagedorn and Leif Hellstrom, *Foreign Invaders — The Douglas Invader in Foreign Military and U.S. Clandestine Service,* Midland Publishing Ltd., Leicester, UK, 1994. [2] Col. Michael E. Haas, USAF (Ret), *Apollo's Warriors — United States Air Force Special Operations during the Cold War,* Air University Press, Maxwell AFB, Alabama, 1997. [3] *Ibid.*

The U.S. Department of Commerce's Weather Bureau operated this customized radar-nosed Invader, registered N800W (44-35725), up to February 1965. It subsequently joined ranks of B-26s at Davis-Monthan Air Force Base, Arizona, where it was photographed in April of 1971. (American Aviation Historical Society photo number 5865)

Yellow-white exhaust residue lightens the glossy black nacelles on a trio of turretless postwar B-26Cs. (Douglas/Harry Gann)

White-bordered red propeller warning band stands out on black Korean War-vintage Invader. Large "USAF" on right wing is red. (Douglas/Harry Gann)

SOUTHEAST ASIA

A WAR OF ANACHRONISMS

As fighting embroiled French colonials and Indochinese insurgents into the early 1950s, A-26s in French markings contributed to the bomb tonnage expended in the ultimately futile effort to keep Indochina—Vietnam—as a French possession. Even as the United States hoped for a peaceful accommodation between the French and Vietnamese nationals, the specter of communism prompted U.S. materiel aid to France. In 1951, the United States provided to France five RB-26s, followed by 24 straight B-26 bomber variants, transported on an aircraft carrier as far as Hawaii, from which they were flown to the French at Tourane. Nine more Invaders intended for French use flew to

Vietnam from Sacramento that year, via Hawaii. America's own needs for Invaders in Korea soon eroded the levels of support that could be given the French.[1]

By January 1954, Viet Minh actions in Laos were met by French pilots in U.S. supplied B-26s. Far East Air Forces (FEAF) gave up 16 Invaders that year, which were flown to Clark Air Base in the Philippines where French markings were applied. These were lent to the French in the first three months of 1954 until an equal number of B-26s, plus three RB-26s, procured under terms of the Mutual Defense Assistance Program (MDAP), reached Indochina. Some American mechanics from FEAF assisted the French in maintaining

their Invaders during this period. Later that spring, 25 more B-26Bs were furnished to aid the French in Indochina. That month, and through 2 May, French B-26s dropped a total of 132 cluster bombs carrying Lazy Dog finned bullets on antiaircraft artillery emplacements. The tiny missiles, smaller than a .50-caliber but larger than a .30-caliber bullet, were packed some 11,000 to a cluster bomb, which opened at 5,000 feet above ground, sending the finned bullet shapes hurtling earthward with lethal speed. French Privateers also joined in the Lazy Dog strikes, which appeared to force the Viet Minh to disperse their AA assets, to the advantage of French aircraft overhead. Lazy Dog strikes against AA guns in the vicinity of

B-26K/A-26A 64-17643, photographed at Andrews Air Force Base in May 1965, crashed on 24 July 1966 during landing at Nakhon Phanom, Thailand, according to records assembled by historian Dan Hagedorn. (Besecker/AAHS collection)

DOUGLAS
A-26 INVADER

Dien Bien Phu aided French resupply efforts there, but ultimately this became the site of a chilling French defeat by 7 May 1954. Recovery of loaned Invaders to Clark Air Base was accomplished by the first week of September, as the French presence in Indochina came to an end.[2]

France's departure coincided with an increase in American involvement in the region; the Invader's war in Southeast Asia was not over, as communist and anti-communist factions maneuvered for advantage there.

Farm Gate

If the B-26 Invader was suited to the kind of combat waged in Southeast Asia in the early 1960s, it had another, more political, qualification that for a time put it well ahead of many combat aircraft possessed by the United States: It was propeller-driven. Terms of the Geneva accords of 1954, intended to peacefully resolve Vietnamese issues, specifically forbade the introduction of jet-powered combat aircraft into the region. For awhile, at least, the United States paid attention to this proviso, electing to send A-26s, A-1s, and armed T-28s to help South Vietnam.

On 14 April 1961, in response to a presidential thrust for each American armed service to prepare an effective counterinsurgency force, the U.S. Air Force formed the 4400th Combat Crew Training Squadron at Eglin Air Force Base, Florida. Nicknamed Jungle Jim, the outfit was charged with the responsibility of training indigenous air forces like the South Vietnamese in the use of B-26s, T-28s, and C-47s in counterinsurgency operations. Initially, eight Invaders were in service with Jungle Jim, with eight more in storage.[3]

The first B-26s of Jungle Jim, typically in gray overall paint schemes, were essentially stock Invaders. A fully loaded Invader had a combat radius of 400 miles with a loiter time of 30 to 45 minutes—a helpful asset in supporting troops in the field. In 1961, the Department of Defense made plans to support the South Vietnamese in their efforts to stop communist pressures against them. Included was the authorization in October to send a detachment from Jungle Jim, to be nicknamed Farm Gate, to South Vietnam to operate four B-26s, eight T-28s, and some C-47s to train Vietnamese fliers while honing and refining American counterinsurgency air support doctrine and tactics. Four gunnose Invaders already in the Far East became the initial Farm Gate complement of B-26s, arriving in Bien Hoa near the end of December 1961.[4] Possibly these initial Farm Gate Invaders came from the aborted Mill Pond contingent of B-26s sent to Thailand in 1961 to counter a North Vietnamese presence in Laos. Mill Pond air strikes were called off before they began, at about the same time the Bay of Pigs invasion in Cuba was having some negative repercussions in the U.S.[5]

The scope and duties of the American Farm Gate crews were initially ill-defined. The crews expect-

This B-26B (44-35525) at Hurlburt Field circa 1962 showed off ammunition and bombs it could carry. (AFHRA)

ed to fly combat; some in the government saw Farm Gate as strictly a tool for training Vietnamese combat crews. In December 1961, direction filtered through PACAF (Pacific Air Forces) to permit American Farm Gate crews to fly combat missions in the Vietnamese-marked Invaders and other warplanes as long as at least one South Vietnamese was aboard the airplane. By early 1962, the eight-gun strafer B-26s were appreciated for the withering fire they could place on

The presence of Americans in combat cockpits over South Vietnam became very public on 3 February 1963 when Viet Cong gunners downed a Farm Gate RB-26, killing Capts. John F. Shaughnessy, Jr., and John P. Bartley. Two Farm Gate Invaders were lost that month; air operations soon switched to doubling up the number of strike aircraft, so when possible, one B-26 could cover another during attack passes, suppressing enemy gunfire. As the year

RB-26s were dispatched to Tan Son Nhut in March 1963, arriving from Fort Worth, Texas. Two of these recon Invaders were RB-26L models, experimentally mounting Reconofax IV infrared sensors and cameras. The ability to sense thermal variations caused by vehicles, campfires and traffic on trails made infrared devices attractive, and increasingly useful as they were developed over time. But the system fitted to the RB-26Ls was originally intended for B-58s.

A-26A 64-17671 (originally 44-35820) returned from Southeast Asia, eventually going on display in Florence, South Carolina by the time the photo was taken in August 1971. (Narland/AAHS collection)

Viet Cong troop concentrations. Some early Farm Gate sorties were flown by B-26s at night, using flare light from a cooperating C-47 to illuminate targets. In the last half of 1962, Farm Gate obtained two RB-26Cs for night reconnaissance work. As late as October 1962, no South Vietnamese pilots were actually in flight training to become B-26 pilots.[6]

progressed, Farm Gate at Bien Hoa became the First Air Commando Squadron on 8 July. By this time, the organization's Invader element consisted of 10 B-26s and two RB-26s at Bien Hoa, plus eight B-26s in detachments at Soc Trang and Pleiku.

To counter Viet Cong nocturnal activity, four more Farm Gate

Humidity and dust fouled the sensors, and as photo flares were ejected from the RB-26L ahead of the infrared installation, the heat of the flares overpowered the sensors and ruined photographs.[7]

When a wing failed on a B-26 during a strike mission on 16 August 1963, plunging two Americans and one Vietnamese to their deaths,

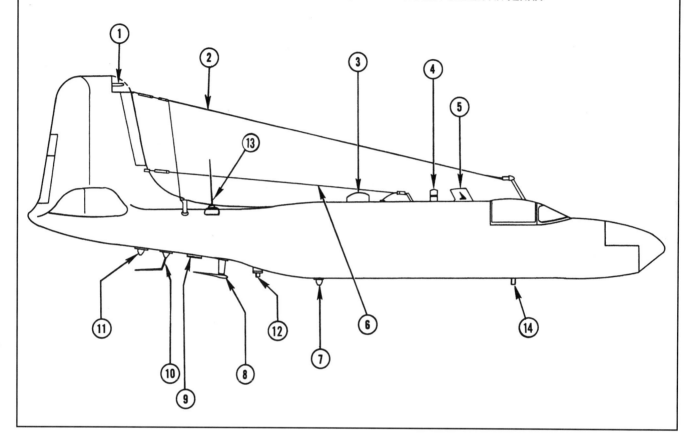

1. AN ARN—14C VOR ILS GLIDE SLOPE ANTENNA
2. HF—103 ANTENNA
3. AN ARN—6 ADF LOOP ANTENNA
4. AN ARC—27 UHF ANTENNA
5. VHF—101 ANTENNA
6. AN ARN—6 ADF SENSE ANTENNA
7. AN APX—25 IFF SIF ANTENNA
8. AN ARN—14C VOR ILS LOCALIZER ANTENNA
9. MARKER BEACON ANTENNA
10. AN ARC—44 FM ANTENNA
11. AN ARN—21C TACAN DISTANCE ANTENNA
12. FM—622 A ANTENNA (BAR) AFTER T.O. 1A—26A—533
13. FM—622 A ANTENNA (WHIP) AFTER T.O. 1A—26A—533
14. RADAR TRANSPONDER ANTENNA

Antenna suite was sophisticated for B-26Ks, as drawn for a technical manual. (Don Keller collection)

the cause was ultimately traced to a quirk originating out of the use of underwing bomb pylons on these Invaders to carry 750-pound bombs. The weight of the wing bombs did not overstress the B-26s in flight, but repeated bouncing over uneven taxiways, ramps, and runways was flexing the wings downward under the heavy bomb loads, hastening their structural fatigue. Farm Gate pilots were told to go easy on their B-26s; back at Van Nuys, California, the On Mark Engineering company was working on a specially beefed-up B-26K variant in an

effort to halt the wing fatigue. The Farm Gate fliers were expected to nurse their aging B-26s until June 1964, when the first of 18 On-Mark B-26Ks with strengthened wings were forecast to arrive. (In actuality, the B-26K was tested in the United States in 1964, and sent to Southeast Asia in 1966.) Tragedy struck again in February 1964 when a wing came off a B-26 in flight at Eglin Air Force Base, Florida, prompting the withdrawal from combat of all B-26s in Vietnam. Though the 34th Tactical Group at Bien Hoa tried to keep the First Air Commando Squadron

Invaders serviceable, widespread cracks and loose rivets told a story of fatigue borne by the B-26s. By early April 1964, the last of the old Farm Gate B-26s and RB-26s were to be gently ferried to Clark AB in the Philippines for scrapping. [8]

Truck Busting

Evaluating data from A-26A Counter Invader missions flown over Laos in 1968 and the first six months of 1969, a consortium of Air Force planners and analysts agreed "that during 1968 and the first six months of 1969 the A-26

destroyed, on the average, about three times as many trucks per attack as the F-4."[9] This highlighted an ongoing Southeast Asia debate about the merits of slow, loitering bomb-haulers like the A-26 and A-1 versus 'fast movers'—jets like the McDonnell F-4 Phantom II.

Ground rules for the study said "if one aircraft in a flight of two expends ordnance against a truck target, two attacks are recorded in the data. If one aircraft attacks two separate truck targets, it is also recorded as two attacks." For the 18 months spanning January 1968 to June 1969, A-26s made 4401 attacks against trucks in Laos, compared with 5850 by F-4s and 2940 by A-1s. This resulted in 2856 trucks destroyed or damaged by A-26s; 1220 by F-4s, and 1021 by A-1s in that time period. Statistically, this equated to 65 trucks destroyed or damaged per 100 attacks by A-26s, compared with 21 for F-4s and 35 for A-1s. [10]

During the last three months of the study period, A-26 truck-busting statistics declined, possibly due to increased anti-aircraft defensive activity, or weather conditions, or to the exhaustion of available stocks of M-36 incendiary ordnance—an effective A-26 munition, particularly for truck-killing. (Invaders used other conventional ordnance in the interim; a study of the lethality of A-26s against trucks noted: "Additional M-36 bombs for the A-26 are currently being produced and should improve the A-26 results.") Even as its averages declined, the A-26 still posted a truck-killing rate 1.4 times that of the F-4.

Using data from the Joint Chiefs of Staff (JCS) Combat Air Activities File (COACT), the study of truck-killing noted an indication "that the propeller aircraft attack more targets per sortie (probably as a result of their ability to remain longer in the target area) than the F-4s," meaning the prop-driven bombers tend-

ed to destroy more trucks per sortie than the fast jets. The study charted dramatic increases in the number of enemy antiaircraft guns in the so-called Steel Tiger area of Laos: "With the incremental cessations of the bombing of North Vietnam there was a notable increase in the number of anti-aircraft guns in the Steel Tiger area …" As confirmed by photo reconnaissance, at the beginning of April 1968, 123 anti-aircraft guns were in that portion of Laos; by the end of the year this had grown to 324 guns. By the first of February 1969, a high of 559 enemy anti-aircraft guns were counted there; this diminished slightly to 490 guns in mid-March and back to 516 anti-aircraft guns of all calibers (23, 37, 57, and 85 millimeter) by the first of July 1969.[11]

The study said A-26s were dispatched primarily at night in part because of the increased anti-aircraft threat. "Nighttime is the period of the most active truck movement," the study noted. The study,

B-26K 61-7640 in flight in August 1964 shows use of bright insignia on glossy green and gray surface; operational USAF Counter Invaders used small insignia if any at all. (U.S. Air Force)

Light-bottomed eight-gun-nose A-26A underwent servicing at On Mark's facility at Van Nuys, California in the late 1960s. Characteristically, Counter Invaders sent into combat had black undersurfaces. (Frederick A. Johnsen)

favoring F-4s in spite of the evidence showing more kills by A-26s, concluded: "… Of the three aircraft, the F-4 provides the only capability to operate in all areas of Laos 24 hours per day."[12]

Here's How It's Done

During the period covered by the Southeast Asia truck-killing study, an A-26 tactics manual was written for the benefit of newly assigned combat Invader crews. Unpublished, it nonetheless survived to be placed in the Air Force archives at Maxwell Air Force Base. Though variety and innovation—hallmarks of American airmen—suggest this manual would not be a universal roadmap of all the Counter Invader tactics used, its narrative nonetheless offers a glimpse into the last American war of the A-26: "The primary mission of the A-26 aircraft of the 56th Special Operations Wing is to provide night armed reconnaissance of hostile lines of communications (LOCs) within the Steel Tiger and Barrel Roll Sectors. As such, this mission is part of an overall interdiction program for these LOCs. In addition, there is a less frequent though equally important mission of providing close air support for friendly ground forces operating within these same areas."[13]

The Steel Tiger area teemed with many aircraft which were usually orchestrated by an airborne Forward Air Controller (FAC); in the spacious Barrel Roll area, "the A-26 is normally its own FAC." The manual said: "In the Steel Tiger area there are many aircraft operating in a relatively small area which necessitates a positive control system for all air strikes." The manual recorded for posterity the role of Counter Invaders in Southeast Asia: "The primary and most lucrative target assigned to the A-26 is hostile trucks moving along the highway system. Immediately following this target in importance are the known truck park and storage areas. Strikes on these targets must be made within the current Rules of Engagement. Since the Rules of Engagement are continually changing and being updated, they will not be discussed in this manual." Airmen were often hobbled by Rules of Engagement over Southeast Asia that had the unintended consequence of broadening the sanctuary enjoyed by the enemy. The A-26 tactics manual summed this with: "The only word of advice concerning the Rules of Engagement is that if you are not certain that a strike is permitted within the specified parameters, then do not make the strike."[14]

The manual touted the A-26's unique characteristics, including long loiter time, low speed capability, large and varied ordnance capacity, and two-man crew, as making the Counter Invader "uniquely suited to the mission of night armed reconnaissance." To enhance their utility at night, Counter Invaders typically flew with black undersurfaces; some early B-26Ks were finished with light undersurfaces for day work.

New crews in Southeast Asia quickly learned a salient difference between combat drops and training sorties back in the U.S. In combat over Southeast Asia, higher bomb release minimums were established. "In order to reduce combat damage and loss of aircraft, a minimum ordnance release altitude of 5,000 feet AGL (Above Ground Level) has been established." The nearly mile high minimums necessitated some additional windage and sight corrections. The manual elaborated: "There are documented cases where the combat loss of an A-26 aircraft and crew was directly attributed to being at too low an altitude. There are no documented cases of a loss being due to too high an altitude. The use of 5,000 feet AGL release altitude is a proper compromise between degradation of accuracy and safety. At 5,000 feet, the aircraft can be hit by hostile ground fire, however this altitude does provide time for either gaining control of the aircraft or abandoning it."[15]

The manual noted: "There are no standardized tactics employed for ordnance delivery in this area. There are, however, some basic principles which have definite application and are proven through successful use to be of value." Crews were told to avoid making rectangular patterns with repeat run-ins from the same direction, because this repetition "will quickly transfer the advantage you have to the defending forces." The manual observed: "You will find that range error is much greater than azimuth (error), consequently 'coming down the road' will increase your probability of a hit on the road. However, do not continually strike on one heading but try 180 degrees to your initial attack. In all cases, when pulling off the target, observe the gun fire pattern and use this information to determine the heading and escape route for subsequent passes. Each pass you make will provide new information concerning the particular defenses in that area. Use your eyes; look around and use what you see to your advantage. You can bet that the defensive forces on the ground are doing the same thing."[16]

A-26 crews were advised to treat all targets as if they were heavily defended, since enemy firepower varied considerably, and there was no way to accurately determine its severity before making an attack.

The Counter Invaders described in the manual used a mixture of ordnance "generalized as a mix of incendiary and fragmentation munitions … The most effective munitions resulting in the greatest number of truck kills and secondary fires has been area incendiary munitions," the manual noted. "One factor in the primacy of these munitions has been the self-imposed ground rule that, barring other considerations, a destroyed truck must be seen burning on or near the highway system. While such a rule does not deny the destructive potential of general purpose and fragmentation munitions, it does weight the evidence in confirmed bomb damage assessment (BDA) reports in favor of the incendiary munitions," according to the manual draft.

Favored among the incendiary devices for Southeast Asia truck busting were M-31 and M-32 incendiary cluster bombs, which dispersed over a large area, with the ability to ignite trucks. The Invader pilots of Steel Tiger and

Ubiquitous gray B-26Bs were stored at Davis-Monthan Air Force Base, Arizona, when photographed in 1971. Openings, gaps and glazing have been sealed with "Spraylat" preservative material. (Frederick A. Johnsen)

Glass-nosed A-26A Counter Invader number 64-17664, in storage in Arizona by 1971, had been part of the Steel Tiger force in late 1966 and most of 1967. This Counter Invader appears to have gray-bottomed glass nose on otherwise black-bottom aircraft, suggesting a post-combat installation. (Frederick A. Johnsen)

Barrel Roll reported coverage by one incendiary cluster to equal that of as many as 20 750-pound napalm bombs. Such broad ground coverage had the added benefit of getting kills even with less than pinpoint accuracy on the part of the Counter Invader crew. But just as this was the last gasp for Invaders in the U.S. Air Force, so too were M-31 and M-32 bombs anachronisms from another era. As the draft manual reported: "These munitions were developed and utilized during World War Two and have not been in production for quite some time. Consequently, the supply is rapidly being depleted." M-31s and M-32s were credited with the best ratio of trucks destroyed per weapons delivered, the manual said.[17]

Finned napalm bombs, designated BLU-23, 27, and 32, "are the second most effective weapons utilized for truck and storage area targets." As with the M-31s and M-32s, these weapons required a bombing sight depression greater than that available in the A-26 when bombing from 5,000 feet. "Even though this is the case, the proper sight picture can easily be visualized and fair accuracy obtained," the manual said.

Unfinned 250-pound BLU-10 napalm canisters lost too much accuracy when released at 5,000 feet AGL. "The instability of these munitions which provides for the spread during low level delivery also produces gross errors when released at higher altitudes with a diving delivery," the manual explained. The BLU-10 as a Counter Invader munition from 5,000 feet was described in the manual as "very effective as a ground mark reference for delivery of other weapons and does have a potential

destructive power if fortune decrees that it impact on the target."[18]

Fragmentation bombs of the M1A4 type were available in sufficient quantity to be readily available for A-26 operations. Less likely to ignite a truck than fire bombs were, the use of M1A4s or other fragmentation bombs made nocturnal damage assessment virtually impossible. But, the manual draft recorded, the potential for damage to the enemy was there: "By dropping three or four M1A4s in a string a relatively large area can be covered with good damage potential for light materiel targets." General purpose bombs— Mk-81s, Mk-82s, and M-117s— could be fuzed in several ways. "Normal fuzing is for a non-delay nose fuze and a 0.025 sec. delay tail fuze," the draft explained. Bombs thusly armed were often selected for use against trucks and

Rows of Counter Invaders and standard B-26s formed a ghostly link with the past at Davis-Monthan Air Force Base's vast storage compound in the late summer of 1971. Three A-26As nearest camera (numbers 657, 658, and 647) were stateside trainers never assigned to Southeast Asia. (Frederick A. Johnsen)

storage areas; bombs armed only with the slightly-delayed tail fuzes were favored when the object was to dig craters in the earth. A nose fuze extender could be used to cause detonation a few feet above the ground if desired. [19]

Cluster bomb munitions such as the CBU-14, CBU-25, CBU-24, CBU-29, and CBU-49 "are very effective as flak suppression weapons," the draft noted, adding: "Of these, the tube dispensing CBU-14 and CBU-25 are the ones most often carried on the A-26." But both of these munitions were devised for low-altitude release, and were inaccurate when dropped from higher altitudes. The CBUs were susceptible to wind drift the higher they were released, but a broad footprint somewhat compensated for this.

A-26s in Southeast Asia by the late 1960s could be their own FACs. Flares and ground marks were available for tube launching from SUU-25 dispensers or MAU-63 racks carried by the bombers. Otherwise, the Counter Invader crews usually worked with a FAC assigned a specific geographic area. New A-26A crews would do well to check and double check the FAC's instructions before making an ordnance delivery run; old hands said the extra time taken to make sure of a target location at night paid off in a higher percentage of targets destroyed. While the use of flares was prevalent in training, in combat, Counter Invader crews in the Steel Tiger region were less likely to do so, because the same flares that illuminated the target made the strike aircraft stand out too. And in marginal weather, flares could contribute to spatial disorientation. Moonlight could permit attacks to be made

without flares or ground markers. The draft noted: "During periods of from one-half through full moon there is normally enough ground illumination to permit easy identification of hard targets (i.e. truck parks, storage areas, etc.) Within the limitation of the Rules of Engagement, the A-26 crew does qualify as a FAC for its own strikes and those made by other aircraft." [20]

Trucks moving at night could be difficult to spot. Their headlights were shielded, but if the beam could be detected it appeared blue-white compared to the red-orange of small fires. Since electrical power was "practically nonexistent" in that combat area, the only electric lights likely to be encountered were those on vehicles. When suspected trucks were found, the best positive identification would come from a FAC

equipped with a starlight scope for night vision.

During night operations, hostile ground fire had to be weighed as a threat. As the manual draft explained: "In general, night operations in Barrel Roll receive very little hostile ground fire. Steel Tiger has a greater concentration of defensive fire power and ground fire can be expected on all strikes." To the gunners' advantage on the ground, multiple batteries would sometimes take turns firing on an aircraft, making it more difficult to spot where the fire came from. Typically antiaircraft gunners from two or more weapons would lay a pattern of converging fire above a target. But the black-bottom A-26As, if they avoided light sources, could maximize their survivability, as the manual draft noted: "An aircraft operating at night, without lights, presents an extremely difficult tar-

get. The end result being that the guns generally fire in the area where you are expected to be but not necessarily where you actually are. During a dark night you have the advantage in that you can see them but they must guess your location. Moonlight will greatly aid the hostile gunners unless you take the precaution to never make a pass down-moon with the moon directly off your tail and never pull off directly into the moon. If there is a bright moon and thin, high overcast the aircraft becomes much more visible and the gunners may be able to optically track the aircraft thus greatly increasing their accuracy." Faced with this combination of moon and silhouetting haze, the Counter Invader draft instructions advised, "first, if the attack must be made, limit your passes to the minimum, second, find another target less heavily defended." [21]

Flak suppression was often desirable; even solo Invaders could select cluster bomb units to sow over gun emplacements while setting up to attack a primary target. Multiple aircraft could cover each other. In flak suppression, one cardinal rule pertained: "Do not attempt to duel barrel to barrel with a ground gun emplacement … If you attempt dueling a ground gun emplacement with your cal. .50 (machine guns) you present a target with zero deflection and greatly increase your probability of being hit." Instead, an aircraft passing by a gun emplacement, and not flying directly toward or away from it presented a constantly moving target. CBUs had another advantage: "The noise of the exploding munitions will, at the minimum, distract the gunners and make it more difficult for them to determine the time of your attack from the sound of the aircraft alone." [22]

Motley paint on A-26A 64-17657 included gray-bottomed tip tank, as seen at Davis-Monthan Air Force Base in September 1971. Stateside A-26As received IF tail code. (Frederick A. Johnsen)

As unnerving as tracer fire could be, the Barrel Roll/Steel Tiger A-26 tactics manual draft advised: "Generally speaking, if you can see a round of tracer coming up it will not hit you. It is always the round that you do not see which hits your aircraft, so attempt to see every round fired and you can be relatively safe." One way to do this was to pull off a target run in a tight climbing turn, getting back up to strike altitude, while keeping the target in sight, watching for tracers, and noting impact of ordnance.

Though the Counter Invaders were intended for visual delivery of ordnance during armed reconnaissance missions, B-26Ks could make use of Combat Sky Spot, a system of high-precision ground-based radar that could direct the Counter Invader on a level bombing run, furnishing the pilot bomb release information. The Invader's SST-181X radar transponder, referred to as "Music" by Combat Sky Spot controllers, was engaged. Feedback from Combat Sky Spot guided the Invader pilot. The manual draft said: "The aircraft must be flown at the prescribed altitude and true airspeed. If bombs are to be delivered from the bomb bay, the doors should be opened not later than two minutes out from the release point in order to permit time for stabilizing the airspeed. The accuracy of this system requires good pilot technique in maintaining requested altitude and airspeed." Ballistics tables were used to predict the release point for Combat Sky Spot-directed bomb drops, so only one type of ordnance could be used per pass. Some cluster bombs and unfinned napalm tanks were unsuitable for this type of blind delivery because of their inherently unpredictable ballistics. Thunderstorm activity could thwart the ability of the ground-based radar. [23]

New Counter Invader pilots in Southeast Asia were warned that enemy forces might listen in on the radio; to avoid giving out compass headings for attack run-ins, some pilots used numbers to designate quadrants of the compass; northwest was 4, northeast 1, southeast 2, and southwest 3. A more demanding (and probably confounding to the enemy) way of noting headings used the various United States to describe a direction of travel, as explained in the Counter Invader draft: "… An aircraft going from Texas to Washington is proceeding in a northwesterly direction."

Sometimes A-26As worked with C-123 or C-130 FACs at night. These large transport aircraft included crewmembers nicknamed scopers and kickers. The scoper used a Starlight night vision device to spot road traffic or other targets; the kickers dropped flares or markers out of the rear of the aircraft as required by the scoper, or the FAC, who was in one of the pilots' seats up front. Ground FACs, often in sight of trucks, also directed some strikes. Language barriers could pose problems since ground FACs were often local nationals; short, simple sentences were the order of the day. [24]

The racehorse A-26 Invader—upgraded as the Counter Invader—bridged the gap between rustic Kentucky-windage bomb release judgment and electronic technology to serve the U.S. Air Force in Southeast Asia a quarter century after its baptism by fire.

Sometime in late 1968 or early 1969, an Air Force egress team was dispatched to Nakon Phanom, Thailand, where they installed Yankee extraction seats in two of the A-26As before the team was taken off that project for other duties. [25]

U.S. Air Force A-26 operations were discontinued in November 1969, with nine A-26As from Tactical Air Command, and one returning aircraft from Southeast Asia, placed in desert storage at Davis-Monthan Air Force Base, Arizona. Five others were released under provisions of the Military Assistance Program for non-flight training purposes, and one was enshrined as a display at Hurlburt Field, Florida. Three VB-26s in the Air National Guard were retired in this time period. Final termination of the B-26 as a logistics and support item occurred 30 June 1970; after that time, it was consigned to countries under the Military Assistance Program.

[1] Robert F. Futrell, with Martin Blumenson, *The United States Air Force in Southeast Asia — The Advisory Years to 1965,* Office of Air Force History, Washington, D.C., 1981. [2] *Ibid.* [3] *Ibid.* [4] *Ibid.* [5] Col. Michael E. Haas, USAF (Ret), *Apollo's Warriors — United States Air Force Special Operations during the Cold War,* Air University Press, Maxwell AFB, Alabama, 1997. [6] Robert F. Futrell, with Martin Blumenson, *The United States Air Force in Southeast Asia — The Advisory Years to 1965,* Office of Air Force History, Washington, D.C., 1981. [7] *Ibid.* [8] *Ibid.* [9] Memorandum For Acting Assistant Secretary of Defense (System Analysis), Subject: "Relative Effectiveness in Truck Killing Role of A-26, A-1, and F-4 Aircraft", 9 Oct 69, kept in AFHRA Archives, Maxwell AFB, Alabama. [10] Study, "Relative Efficiency of F-4, A-1, and A-26 Aircraft Attacking Trucks in Laos," by OSD (Systems Analysis), and Air Staff (AFXDC, AFGOA, and AFCSA), 1969. [11] *Ibid.* [12] *Ibid.* [13] *AFLC Tactics Manual — A-26A* (unpublished), written November 1968, (AFHRA, Maxwell AFB, Alabama). [14] *Ibid.* [15] *Ibid.* [16] *Ibid.* [17] *Ibid.* [18] *Ibid.* [19] *Ibid.* [20] *Ibid.* [21] *Ibid.* [22] *Ibid.* [23] *Ibid.* [24] *Ibid.* [25] Interview, author with CMSgt. Doug Nelson, USAF (Ret), 10 June 1998.

INVADER COLOR

When first flown, the A-26 entered an Army Air Forces world of olive drab and gray that persisted into early production Invaders. Soon, freed of the requirement for camouflage, Douglas built A-26Bs and Cs in natural metal finish, commonly seen on World War Two combat Invaders.

As night interdiction using radar, flares, and other tools, gained favor in the postwar Air Force, many Invaders adopted a glossy black paint scheme, with most lettering in red. This pertained to large numbers of Korean War B-26s, although over Korea, mixed formations of silver and black Invaders have been recorded often on film.

By the time Farm Gate B-26s were employed in Viet Nam in the early 1960s, finishes typically were gray or silver paint, sometimes with the formality of South Vietnamese national insignia. A resurgence of Air Force interest in camouflage around 1965 saw earth tones applied or at least proposed for nearly every type of aircraft in the inventory. The remanufactured B-26K Counter Invader received a southeast Asia patchy tan and green camouflage scheme; a few were painted glossy gray overall in the U.S. (possibly Federal Standard color 16473). Specifications for USAF B-26K camouflage upper surfaces called for Federal Standard colors 30219 (tan); 34079 (green); and 34102 (green). Initially, 36622 (gray) was used for the under surfaces, but combat Counter Invaders in southeast Asia received dull black undersides.

Perhaps the greatest variety in A-26 paint schemes appeared on the civilian models, not constrained by military considerations. Bright, readily visible colors adorned fire bombers, while speedlines and dapper trim set off business conversions of the Invader.

First B-26K Counter Invader received by the Air Force was renumbered 61-7640, and arrived in a two-tone green and gray camouflage that looked a lot like an On Mark business paint scheme, with glossy paint and hard demarcation between colors. Though variations on this scheme served foreign air forces, USAF Counter Invaders in combat wore flat variegated camouflage schemes. This 1964 photo depicts the first K-model, following the YB-26K, fitted with three 750-pound napalm canisters and one 250-gallon fuel tank under each wing. (U.S. Air Force)

B-26K 61-7640 in flight in August 1964 shows use of bright insignia on glossy green and gray surface; operational USAF Counter Invaders used small insignia if any at all. (U.S. Air Force)

With one blue exception, a line of brilliant yellow B-26 fire bombers slumbers in Canadian snows between fire seasons. Eleven air tankers of Alberta's 'Airspray' company can be counted in the photo. (Courtesy Airspray Ltd.)

Canada's Airspray fire bomber number 14, Hasta Luego, used a shortened red propeller warning band and a logo depicting winged horses moving an antique fire pumper. Retardant tank doors are open in the photo. (Courtesy Airspray Ltd.)

WARBIRD**TECH**
SERIES

Combat veteran A-26A (B-26K) Counter Invader at Nakhon Phanom, Thailand, circa 1969, shows tan patches on modified nacelles (with recessed dorsal inlets). (George J. Marrett)

Red and gray Phillips Petroleum B-26B (44-34770; N67814) with airstair ladder entering former bomb bay area carried dual ADF "football" antennas on top and bottom of aft fuselage. (Phillips Petroleum collection)

A Tulsa-built A-26B with early-style canopy executed a training mission out of Florence, SC, circa 1945. Pacific combat evaluators criticized this canopy configuration for its limited lateral view over the huge nacelles; 9th Air Force users of early Invaders were less harsh. (Harry Gann)

Face and lettering, Are you one too?, *adorned the six-gun nose of a 12th Bomb Group A-26B in India at the end of World War Two, too late to see combat there. (12th Bomb Group Association)*

A-26A 64-17653 at Davis-Monthan AFB storage facility on 21 September 1971 shows red prop warning stripes, and red indications around hand holds and extendable ladder. This veteran of Southeast Asia combat subsequently was put in the Pima Air Museum in Tucson, Arizona. (Kenneth G. Johnsen)

During the Korean war, 17th Bomb Group pilot Robert C. Mikesh (right) and crew posed with B-26B Monie, *named for Mikesh's wife. (Courtesy Robert C. Mikesh)*

CIVILIAN INVADERS

Abundant in the postwar marketplace, Douglas A-26s have been used as executive transportation, fire bombers, research testbeds, and even in air racing—quite a compliment for a multi-engine bomber. A few A-26s became civilian property in the late 1940s, but a groundswell of civil registrations for Invaders shows up in 1954, after the end of the Korean War. A second increase in the available civilian Invader population took place in the early 1960s.

On Mark Civil Conversions

The On Mark Engineering Company blossomed in the postwar 1950s, firmly associated with the Douglas B-26 Invader from the outset of the company in 1954. Created by Robert O. Denny and L.A. Keithley at the Van Nuys, California, airport, On Mark Engineering secured exclusive licensing rights from Douglas Aircraft for production of Invader spare parts. From this perch, the young company gained a reputation for rebuilding Invaders as corporate aircraft, as well as servicing components on B-26s still in U.S. Air Force service.

The On Mark Marketeer was a remanufactured B-26 Invader which could be fitted with uprated R-2800 engines and outfitted to meet customer specifications. Its useful load of 12,000 pounds could include as many as 11 passengers and a crew of two. The Marketeer's distinctive wingtip fuel tanks were to become a signature of On Mark Engineering, carrying through with various projects including the heavily armed military B-26K Counter Invader of the early 1960s.[1]

To tame the roar of the bomber, the Marketeer's cabin was fitted with double-paned windows, soundproofing, and insulation. Hydraulic airstairs could be fitted either on the right side or under the fuselage; baggage was stowed in the longer nose compartment made

On Mark B-26 conversion for Diamond Match company, photographed 18 November 1957, used fixed tip tanks. Nose contours appear modified from earlier photos of this business aircraft. (Chal Johnson via Peter M. Bowers)

for the Marketeer. Disc brakes and optional reversible-pitch propellers updated the performance of the dual-control Marketeer.[2]

In January 1961, the entrepreneurs of On Mark received a Supplemental Type Certificate for the Marksman, a further-altered iteration of the B-26 Invader billed as a six-to-eight passenger executive transport with a redesigned pressurized fuselage that had higher headroom than a traditional Invader. The Marksman's cockpit featured a Douglas DC-7-type bird-proof heated windscreen and side windows; cabin windows also were like those of the DC-7. A significant change to the Marksman was creation of a steel carry-through for the rear wing spar, redesigned to pass overhead in the cabin, giving more headroom than the original A-26 design. By 1962, a cabin altitude of 6,800 feet could be maintained by versions of the Marksman, while flying as high as 20,000 feet.[3]

The pointed snout attached to the Marksman measured eight feet, seven inches in length, and could accommodate weather radar as well as baggage. Control surfaces were covered in synthetic Ceconite fabric. Options on the Marksman included a new nosewheel steering system and a larger metal rudder. DC-6 wheels were another option.

In the first part of 1964, On Mark Engineering introduced an interesting variation to its pressurized Marksman offerings when

Inspecting an On Mark executive B-26 on 1 February 1957 were Donna Cole, right, and Clay Orum, chief pilot for Humphrey Gold Corporation, providing size comparisons in the bomber's fuselage. Facing aft, the two passengers have a television screen behind them for the benefit of passengers facing them. (On Mark via the San Diego Aerospace Museum)

a cargo door about three feet by five and a half feet was placed in the aft belly of the airplane, opening the pressurized cabin. With the articulated door folding inward against the aft pressure bulkhead, this Marksman version was said to be able to air-drop cargo at speeds up to 310 miles an hour. With high-density seating installed, this Marksman could carry 12 passengers in addition to its crew of two. The Marksman Model C (most, if not all, Marksman examples built were C-models) had a top cruising speed of 365 miles an hour at 23,000 feet.[4] (A-26 chroniclers Dan Hagedorn and Leif Hellstrom say a pair of airdrop-capable Marksmen were used by the Central Intelligence Agency in the mid-1960s over Laos, and may have been the first operational aircraft with terrain-following radar.)

On Mark Engineering typified

On Mark offered Hytrol anti-skid brakes, DC-6 wheels, and chromed landing gear struts on its Invader executive conversions in the 1950s. (On Mark via the San Diego Aerospace Museum)

post-World War Two American aviation companies—innovative, willing to take a risk, and able to see a profitable future in surplus warplanes of the not-too-distant past, years before any of these aircraft would gain status as restored warbirds.

Bill Odom flew the Reynolds Bombshell (NX67834) in 1948. Given an executive conversion the following year by Southwest Airmotive in Dallas, Texas, this Invader served several corporate customers under different civil registration numbers. It was reported to be out of service by 1986. (Bowers collection)

Phillips Petroleum's N666 (44-34754) featured picture windows and a righthand airstair door. Dorsal fin has been shortened slightly at front where it meets recontoured fuselage. (Phillips Petroleum collection)

Squared paddle props and tip tanks graced the Phillips Petroleum B-26 N666. Chromed nosewheel strut glints in the sun. (Phillips Petroleum collection)

LAS Super 26

Lockheed Air Service—LAS—of Ontario, California, went beyond its parent company's products to produce a much-modified Douglas A-26 executive version, the Super 26. Fitted with a more capacious cabin structure, the LAS Super 26 was a six-to-nine-place pressurized aircraft capable of keeping an 8,000-foot cabin altitude up to 20,000 feet. A replacement steel rear spar

High overwing windows and lower picture windows in aft fuselage lend spacious feeling to otherwise cramped quarters in Phillips Petroleum's customized B-26 N666. View is looking aft. (Phillips Petroleum collection)

carry-through ring structure provided more head room. A galley and lavatory could be incorporated in the fuselage. And, where On Mark favored Douglas airliner windows, the Lockheed Air Service Super 26 was said to employ Constellation-type cabin windows. A Lockheed-designed Fiberglass nose housed electronics and baggage, and access was eased by use of an electrically operated airstair door. [5]

L.B. Smith Tempo

Another name in the Invader executive aircraft marketplace into the 1960s was the L.B. Smith company of Miami, Florida. Offerings included the modified Tempo I and pressurized Tempo II, with enlarged fuselages, and the ultimate of the Smith line (in length), the Biscayne 26. [6]

The Smith Tempo II used a new alloy spar to create more cabin space, and which also made a wider stub at the fuselage, increasing wingspan by three feet, five and a half inches (about two feet of which was due to the wing stubs; the rest due to the tip tanks). This had the added benefit of widening the aircraft's landing gear track, said to improve handling. Among features of the Tempo II was the ability to mount JATO bottles for takeoffs from high-altitude airfields. [7]

Rhodes Berry Silver Sixty

In the summer of 1960, another southern California firm, the Rhodes Berry Company, of Los Angeles, flew the prototype of its Silver Sixty A-26 conversion. Where other Invader converters had

(Above and Below): *Alternate paint scheme on Phillips Petroleum's B-26 N666 incorporated dark nacelles; exhaust smudging was always evident on the big Invader nacelles.* (Bowers collection)

employed new spar carry-through members to give more headroom, the Rhodes Berry effort left the top half of the fuselage alone and replaced the lower portion with a deeper structure, resulting in a business aircraft that had a beefier, deeper fuselage sitting closer to the ground than on a stock A-26, without altering the original spar carry-through structure. With head room of about six-and-a-half feet, the Silver Sixty also had a usable cabin length of 22 feet, and was said to be able to carry up to 14 passengers in two rows of single seats divided by a slim 14-inch aisle. A cargo version with rear ventral loading ramp was also planned by Rhodes Berry engineers.[8] According to a contemporary aviation industry journal, the company at one time envisioned a troop-carrier variant that was to have accommodated 20 soldiers, and was intended for the South American market.[9]

The deeper lower fuselage of the Silver Sixty permitted the nosewheel to be stowed without turning it flat as on a standard A-26, and this was said to improve takeoff performance because the aircraft no longer had to endure having the large nosewheel pancaking into the slipstream, producing extra drag during climbout.

LeTourneau Conversions

Following three successful in-house conversions of Invaders for its own far-flung corporate needs, the R.G. LeTourneau company of Longview, Texas, offered similar conversions for other corporate owners in about 1959. More conservative than other deep-fuselaged, re-sparred business B-26s, the LeTourneau modification left the original big rear wing spar in place, while lightening the Invader of unneeded military equipment, and installing passenger accommodations. A finished LeTourneau B-26 had an empty weight of 22,000 pounds—not much under the military empty weight—while retaining the military B-26's gross weight limit of 35,000 pounds, for a load of 13,000 pounds.[10]

The LeTourneau company, whose primary business was manufacturing heavy equipment for industries including petroleum, construction, and logging, used its own converted B-26s to support activities in the United States as well as South America and western Africa. Since LeTourneau conversions were not pressurized, oxygen masks were provided at each seat—a necessity for conducting business over the Andes. With more fuel tanks inside the wings, one of LeTourneau's business B-26s boasted a 3,000-mile range with a fuel reserve sufficient for 45 minutes more.[11]

Among the various Invaders at one time registered in the U.S. to the LeTourneau company were A-26B 44-34134 (civil registration N115RG); A-26B 43-22275 (N114RG); A-26 N4973N; A-26C 44-35949 (N67165); and possibly A-26B 41-39418 (N116R or N116RG) and A-26B 39437 (N117R or N117RG).[12]

Shiny Caribbean Air Transport A-26C (44-35956), with nickname 'Caribbean Queen' lettered on the aft part of the nacelle, carried Bendix race number 45 on the nacelle under the wing (obscured by exhaust in the photo) in 1946. Its civil registration was NX37482. (Gordon S. Williams via Peter M. Bowers)

N4974N's paint scheme in this 1956 photo suggests it was one of the LeTourneau conversions, although its civil registration is one number higher than published LeTourneau registrations. (Don Keller collection)

Grand Central

In the early 1950s, Grand Central Aircraft at Glendale, California, undertook the executive conversion of at least one A-26B, 44-34768 (N4852V). The availability of speedy surplus A-26s doubtless inspired other companies to convert Invaders as well.

Monarch

Civil registration lists of A-26s occasionally reference Rock Island Monarch civilian conversions, generally externally stock-looking machines.

Et Cetera

Modifications to modifications led to a tri-motor B-26; Garrett Airesearch flew an On Mark executive conversion with a turboprop engine in the nose as a flying engine testbed in the early 1980s. One of the earliest executive Invaders may have been A-26C (civil number N67148) modified by Aero Trades Incorporated in New York circa 1951.

Invader N5052N may be an early Lockheed Air Service (LAS) upgrading used by owners including Mesta Machine Co. of Pittsburgh, Pennsylvania, circa 1954. (Don Keller collection)

Fighting Fire

In 1960, the first conversions of Douglas B-26s hit the American firelines as air tankers even as B-25s were being withdrawn for use as fire bombers in California that same year. [13]

Ultimately, a number of U.S. operators flew A-26s as fire bombers, pre-dominantly in the American west, but sometimes into the south as deep as Tennessee. Agricultural and firefighting A-26 users included: Aero Union Corporation, Chico, California; Butler Aircraft, Redmond, Oregon; Central Air Service, East Wenatchee, Washington; D&D Aero Spraying, Rantoul, Kansas; Donaire Incorporated, Phoenix, Arizona; Evergreen Air, Missoula, Montana;

Flick Aviation, LaGrande, Oregon; Flight Enterprises, Prescott, Arizona; Johnson Flying Service, Missoula, Montana; Kinney Air Tankers, Richey, Montana; Lynch Flying Service, Billings, Montana; Reeder Flying Service, Twin Falls, Idaho; and Rosenbalm Aviation, Medford, Oregon.[14] Though generally assigned to a particular air tanker base during the fire season, nomadic fire bombers often were shifted to hot spots for brief periods of high activity, putting Invaders all over the territory.

North of the U.S. border, Conair Aviation in British Columbia operated a fleet of firebombing Invaders in the 1970s, selling their A-26s in the mid-1980s. Air Spray Limited of Edmonton, Alberta, also operated Invaders in this role.

Off to the Races

John Lear raced A-26 (civil registration N3328G) around the pylons in the 1968 National Championship Air Races at Reno, Nevada, after a vote of the other pilots allowed a waiver to the races' traditional gross weight limit of 21,000 pounds. Painted white and bearing the large race number 76 in black on the tail, and the upper left wing, the Invader ran fifth in the consolation race, its average speed of 283.68 miles an hour easing past one of the more traditional Mustang fighters also in the consolation laps. [15]

Two years later, with Lear as copilot and Wally McDonnell in the left seat, A-26 (civil registration N2852G) was a glossy black entrant in the California 1,000 Air Race, roaring repetitively around the course at Mojave. Carrying race number 4, this Invader placed 12th (ironically behind a DC-7 airliner, which, by virtue of its large fuel capacity, flew the 1,000 mile air race nonstop to a sixth place finish). [16]

A few other Invaders, before and since, flew long-distance or endurance races.

[1] Leonard Bridgman and John W.R. Taylor, *Jane's All the World's Aircraft — 1958-59,* McGraw-Hill, New York, 1958. [2] *Ibid.* [3] John W.R. Taylor, *Jane's All the World's Aircraft — 1962-63,* McGraw-Hill, New York, 1962. [4] John W.R. Taylor, *Jane's All the World's Aircraft — 1964-65,* McGraw-Hill, New York, 1964. [5] John W.R. Taylor, *Jane's All the World's Aircraft — 1961-62,* McGraw-Hill, New York, 1961. [6] Rene J. Francillon, *McDonnell Douglas Aircraft Since 1920,* Putnam, London, 1979. [7] John W.R. Taylor, *Jane's All the World's Aircraft — 1963-64,* McGraw-Hill, New York, 1963. [8] John W.R. Taylor, *Jane's All the World's Aircraft — 1961-62,* McGraw-Hill, New York, 1961. [9] "Silver Sixty B-26 Conversion Starts Tests," *Aviation Week,* (circa 1960). [10] Craig Lewis, "LeTourneau to Offer B-26 Conversion," *Aviation Week,* 16 March 1959. [11] *Ibid.* [12] John Chapman and Geoff Goodall, *Warbirds Worldwide Directory,* Warbirds Worldwide, Mansfield, England, 1989. [13] William T. Larkins, "Forest Fire Air Attack System," *American Aviation Historical Society Journal,* Vol. 9, No. 3, Fall 1964. [14] John Chapman and Geoff Goodall, *Warbirds Worldwide Directory,* Warbirds Worldwide, Mansfield, England, 1989. [15] Jim Larsen, *Directory of Unlimited Class Pylon Air Racers,* American Air Museum, Inc., Kirkland, Washington, 1971. [16] *Ibid.*

Several times in the history of the Abbotsford, British Columbia, International Air Show, resident Conair B-26 fire bombers were launched during a pause in the show to fight fires in nearby Canadian forests. Tanker 23 (C-GHLK; 44-34313), formerly Butler Aircraft's tanker A20, built up speed on the Abbotsford show line runway in August 1977 during the air show. Later, this Invader joined an Alberta, Canada, museum. (Frederick A. Johnsen)

Deep-bellied Rhodes Berry Super 60, photographed in 1963, enjoyed roomy cabin and simplified nosewheel retraction. (Smalley/Peltzer/Sommerich/Bowers collections)

High cabin is evident on this much-modified Smith Tempo A-26C (N4204A; 44-35640), photographed with a stock Invader at Van Nuys, California, in the late 1960s. This conversion went through several owners before crashing while serving the University of Nevada for weather research in February 1980. (Frederick A. Johnsen)

With RB-26 side window intact in its nose, Invader N3428G was an early fire bomber conversion operated by Rosenbalm Aviation at Medford, Oregon, circa 1963-72. It was photographed at Medford in the early 1970s. Hatch in bottom of bombardier's nose is open in the photo. (Frederick A. Johnsen)

B-26B N71Y (41-39497) was originally operated by Standard Oil Company as early as 1954 before passing through several owners. (Bowers collection)

Tanker 56 (N86469; 43-22511), operated by Aeroflight, was photographed at Troutdale, Oregon, circa 1967. Extended flaps reveal airflow deflectors. (Frederick A. Johnsen)

Tanker C29, an A-26C (44-35217; N4820E) flew for Flight Enterprises of Prescott, Arizona, when photographed during a test drop in the early 1960s. Later under Canadian registration, this fire bomber Invader crashed near Calgary, Alberta, in July 1984. (Ken Shake)

N237Y, a B-26B (41-39516) modified with elongated nose, tip tanks, picture windows, fuselage recontouring, and clipped dorsal fin, served Standard Oil Company and several owners including Cornell Aeronautical Laboratories' Calspan operation. (Bowers collection)

WARBIRD**TECH**
S E R I E S

Hastily painted out insignia, and daubed-on registration (N4060A), marked a black Invader as it was released from surplus. It was photographed at Teterboro, New Jersey circa 1958. By the early 1970s this B-26B (44-34102) was operated by Lynch Air Tankers as Tanker 01; it reportedly crashed in Kentucky fighting a fire in 1983. (Bowers collection)

For years in the 1960s and 1970s, a nearly stock black RB-26C (N7656C; 44-35444) was kept by Vance Roberts at Boeing Field in Seattle, Washington. Said to be used for occasional high priority freight runs for the Boeing Company, this Invader later became Canadian air tanker number 4 operated by Air Spray Ltd., Edmonton, Alberta, under Canadian registration C-FTFB. (Frederick A. Johnsen)

From fire bomber to warbird air show attraction, B-26B serial 41-39359, fitted with a glass nose, was operated by Jerry Janes under Canadian registration when photographed at Arlington, Washington, in the late 1980s before warbird collector Bob Pond acquired it. It previously was Conair air tanker 21 (C-FBMR). In the 1960s it had been owned by Aero Union of Chico, California, under U.S. registration N91281. (Sharon Lea Johnsen)

This Tulsa-built B-26C N9400Z (44-35905) had an extended belly with a somewhat-streamlined skirt behind it. The aircraft was said to be used for hauling fish during the mid-1960s. (Harry Gann via Peter M. Bowers)

WARBIRD**TECH**
S E R I E S

Fire retardant dump doors can be seen open on a Conair B-26 undergoing maintenance at Abbotsford, British Columbia in the 1970s. (Frederick A. Johnsen)

Large former Royal Canadian Air Force Liberator hangars at Abbotsford, British Columbia, served as the maintenance facility for Conair firebombers including B-26 tanker 30, photographed in the 1970s. Gunner's compartment side door is open; gunner's overhead Plexiglas has been painted silver. (Photo by Frederick A. Johnsen)

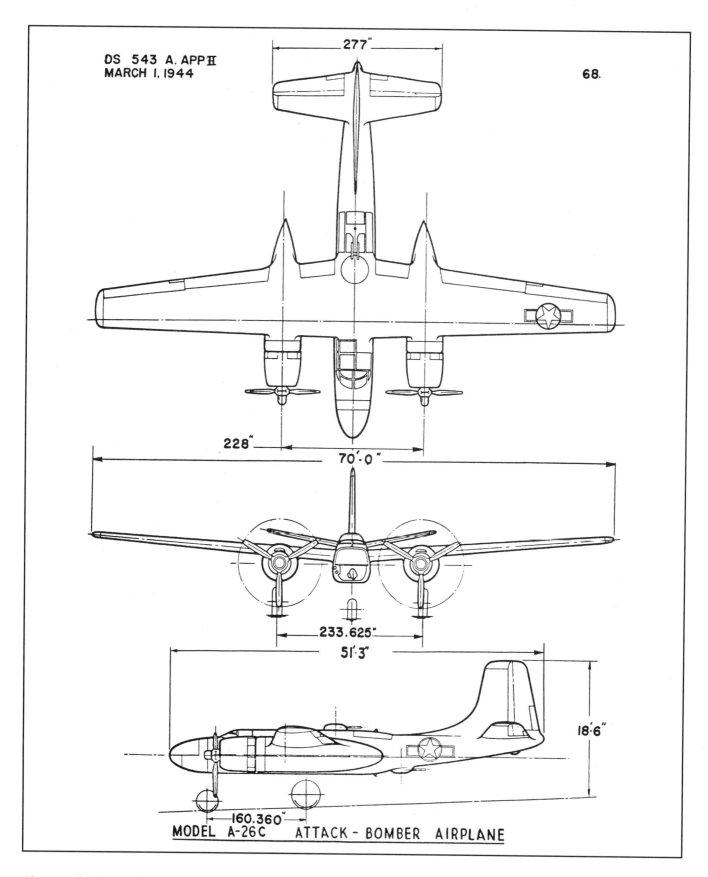

DS 543 A. APP Ⅱ
MARCH 1, 1944

68.

277"

228"

70'·0"

233.625"

51'·3"

18'·6"

160.360"

MODEL A-26C ATTACK - BOMBER AIRPLANE

Line art depicts early A-26C with glass bombardier nose. Some C-model noses could mount a pair of fixed .50-caliber machine guns on the right side. Early low-profile canopy includes ribbed hatch over right side of cockpit. (Douglas/Harry Gann)

BOMBS ACROSS THE SEA

The sporty-looking Douglas A-26 Invader twin-engine bomber was fast, capable, and available, when the U.S. Army Air Forces wanted to try a variation on Barnes Wallis' legendary spherical water-skipping bomb in 1945. Between 4 March and 8 May, as war in Europe raced to an Allied victory, tests were conducted and evaluated at Eglin Field, Florida. The USAAF testers described the bomb: "The test item is 'Speedee' [formerly known as Highball], a British munition weighing 1260-lbs. and carrying a Torpex charge of 600-700-lbs. It is basically spherical in shape with flattened sides and is revolved in the bomb bay by an air turbine

The flat-sided, spherical Speedee bombs test-dropped from an A-26C in 1945 carried contrasting markings to depict their rotation and movement when released. (U.S. Army Air Forces)

at a speed of 800-900 rpm. The direction of rotation is opposite to airplane wheel rotation. Designed for minimum altitude high speed release on water, a long series of ricochets is obtained, with the gyro-

scopic effect of the rotary movement acting to keep the munition on a true course. Upon striking a ship target, the munition should either penetrate or should sink down beside it, maintaining con-

tact while sinking." Speedee was fuzed with a hydrostatic as well as a 60-second self-destructor fuze.[1]

The USAAF was interested in this British device because it promised increased release range with no sacrifice in accuracy, compared with traditional low-level ship bombing tactics. Speedee's touted ability to remain in contact with a ship hull as it submerged after impacting the ship promised damaging detonation near the bottom of armored hulls.

An A-26C was modified for the Speedee tests by cutting holes in

Row of Speedee bombs in wooden cradle awaited trials in Florida waters in the spring of 1945. (U.S. Air Force)

the Invader's flat-bottomed bomb bay doors. In this way, the round bombs could be carried and released without opening the bomb bay doors. Objective of the tests was to learn the general operational effectiveness and the best tactics for use of Speedee, while determining the operational suitability of the Speedee installation in the A-26. [2]

The testers said: "The A-26 type airplane is the only current AAF airplane combining the speed, maneuverability and load-carrying features required for successful adaptation to 'Speedee' attack." A glass-nosed C-model Invader was selected for the Florida tests of Speedee because it afforded a

place for an observer to ride in the nose of the bomber. However, had Speedee gone to war in an A-26, the testers said the added firepower of a gun-nose variant of the Invader like the A-26B "is definitely desirable." [3]

The cutout bomb bay doors and the gyroscopic action of the spinning bombs in the A-26 had no noticeable effect on the bomber's flight characteristics. According to an AAF report: "The test airplane went through steep climbs, turns, and dives normally, with two munitions revolving at full rpm in the bomb bay."

The typical release of a Speedee bomb from the A-26C was

described by the testers: "Contacts with the water are brief and shallow in general, with the travel between successive impacts tending to decrease as speed reduces. The end of the run is a long plough along the surface of the water with the munition sinking at 70 to 90 mph. RPM loss is gradual and the residual rpm at sink normally exceeds 50 percent of initial RPM." [4] The distance of munition travel, height of each skip into the air, and the number of impacts all were interrelated and affected by the condition of the water over which the Speedee munition was released. The AAF noted: " On calm water, low ricochets, a high number of impacts, and a long run result. As roughness of water surface increas-

es, ricochet altitudes also increase while range and number of impacts decrease. Increased severity of impact on a rough water surface causes a higher ricochet with greater loss of forward speed and a harder succeeding impact." The testers said rough-water releases provided greater variation in results, since the angle of a wave as it was hit by the Speedee affected its ricochet and subsequent travel. "On all of the poorer runs, severe first impacts resulted in a high first ricochet, and a relatively quick end to the run."[5]

Particularly over smooth water, lower release altitudes had the effect of prolonging the range the munition traveled before sinking. It was understood that optimum bomb release would take place in level flight following a dive to build up airspeed; if the release was made while the A-26 was still descending in its dive, the downward movement of the bomber had the effect of increasing Speedee's downward velocity, mimicking the effects of dropping from a higher altitude.

For the tests over Florida waters, the A-26C was flown at a calculated indicated airspeed ranging from 360 to 400 miles an hour during weapon release, at altitudes above the water that did not exceed 35 feet, and were often intentionally lower. The majority of 36 releases of Speedee for this test showed that the munition "holds a true course throughout the run along the track of the airplane at release. No measurable deviations occurred on 25 runs," the test report noted. One rough-water release, however, produced an unexplained 185-foot deviation.

Clearance between the bounding bomb and the release aircraft concerned the testers, who noted a minimum safety margin of 26 feet between the bomber and the bomb after first impact when released at about 30-35 feet above the water. This clearance diminished as the A-26 released at lower

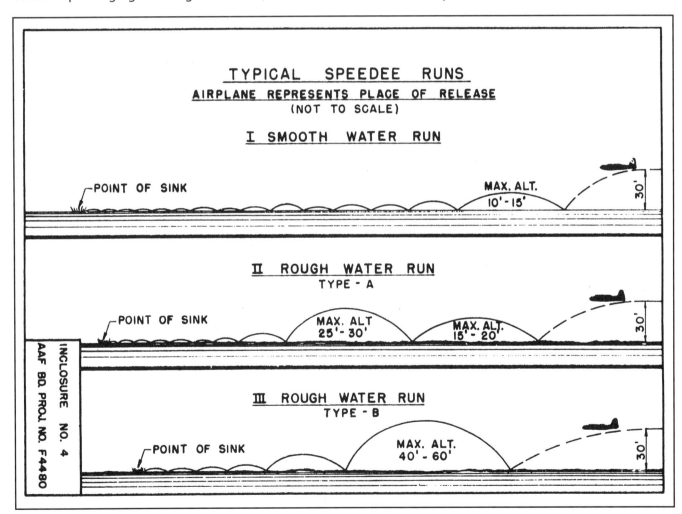

An AAF report depicted Speedee bomb ricochet patterns over the water.

View up into the modified A-26C's bomb bay, with cutout bomb bay doors open, shows ram air turbine at lower left. The turbine spun the bombs as they rode inside the A-26, to impart gyroscopic stability to them long after the munitions were released. The trial Speedee A-26 installation did not lend itself to quick reversion to standard bomber configuration. (U.S. Air Force)

Openings cut in Speedee A-26's bomb bay doors allowed the slightly protruding round bombs to be released without opening the doors. Air turbine duct beneath bomb bay supplied ram air to spin the bombs prior to release, for added stability. (U.S. Air Force)

heights, until at a height of only 11 to 15 feet above the water, Speedee came within four feet of the belly of the bomber on its first rebound. The Speedee report noted: "No clearances less than four to five feet were experienced until 24 April when three releases were made at six to 10 feet, substantially lower than any previous releases. One release cleared by three feet, one by 10 feet, and the last appeared to pass within one-half foot of the airplane." This last release smacked hard into a wave, sending an unforgiving water splash up to the belly of the A-26, denting the fuselage and damaging the modified bomb bay doors. Release minimums were thereafter set at 15 feet. The time from release until Speedee reached the target was typically between 10 and 16 seconds. [6]

Testers suggested the bomber should continue on course after releasing Speedee to avoid presenting a bottom profile to enemy gunners on the targeted ship, saying: "A sharp turn immediately after release is practicable, but trial runs proved that, at 1,600 yards release range, the attacking airplane must still come within 600 to 800 yards of the target." As an alternative, the bomber could "pull up slightly and carry out a strafing run on the target, then withdrawing on the deck." [7]

Tragedy gripped the Speedee program on 28 April when the pilot, according to an AAF report, "probably without realizing it, released at nine to 10 feet. Water conditions were rough (two to three foot waves) and the munition ricocheted up fast after a very severe impact. It struck the airplane aft of the belly turret and emerged in the vicinity of the tail surfaces, the entire tail structure then breaking off." The hapless A-26 immediately pitched down and smashed into the water within a half second, disintegrating in a high-speed crash. Planned comparisons pitting range and speed of the Speedee-equipped A-26 with a standard Invader went unfulfilled following the loss of the test aircraft. [8]

In the aftermath of the Speedee A-26 tests and crash, the Eglin team assessed the radical spherical munition: "In accuracy, 'Speedee' can be expected to fall short of low level bombing, since the probable increase in deflection error will more than counterbalance the greater ease of solving the range problem." When compared to torpedo bombing, the overall aiming problem on moving targets was simplified with Speedee by the reduction in elapsed time from release to target, "but on stationary targets in harbors, the problem is substantially the same" with torpedoes or Speedee bombs, the testers reported. [9]

A torn and wrinkled cutout bomb bay door, plus other sheet metal damage, was the result of an unexpectedly powerful water column slamming up into the Speedee-dropping A-26 on 24 April 1945. (U.S. Air Force)

The Speedee test installation was not readily interchangeable with standard A-26 bomb racks, and testers said unless quick interchangeability could be devised, this trait would limit the versatility of Speedee bombers. They noted: "The use of 'Speedee' is also restricted to water targets and the airplane cannot be used for normal bomb loads [without swapping out rack installations]. The actual 'Speedee' load is equivalent to two 1,000-pound G.P. (general purpose) bombs, or only 50 per cent of the A-26 type airplane's capacity." [10]

On the plus side of the ledger, Speedee's overwater skipping delivery promised to thwart underwater torpedo nets found in some harbors. And, "the characteristic low ricochets over the last part of the [Speedee] munition's run should offer a better chance of close underwater detonation than the bombing attack, which will fail if delivered outside the limits of a fairly narrow effective release range." While Speedee showed promise for armored ship attacks, and had reasonable potential for other surface shipping targets, the Eglin testers said the spherical munitions "showed no indication of being superior to low level and/or torpedo attack" for typical non-armored surface shipping.

The testers worded a warning for any future A-26 Speedee missions that might be undertaken: "Release altitudes should never be lower than 30 feet owing to the possibility of the first ricochet striking the airplane when water conditions are rough. Future installations should have an automatic altitude limit warning device." With the European war at an end as the report was prepared, the Eglin testers said: "It is doubtful whether there are in the Pacific enough [appropriate] targets … which cannot be handled with already available weapons to make the use of 'Speedee' an urgent requirement. In this connection, 'Speedee's' lack of adaptability to other loads and other types of attack also carries weight." Nonetheless, further tests were urged. [11]

Speedee's moment of fame was brief in the USAAF test world. But it pointed out the traits of Yankee ingenuity—adaptability and curiosity—that made the USAAF a war-winner, and the inventiveness, determination and cooperation that cast the Royal Air Force and the British aviation establishment in that same role.

[1] Letter, HQ AAF Proving Ground Command, Eglin Field, Florida, to CO, Flight Test Section, 610th AAF Base Unit, H, Eglin Field, Florida, Subject: Program for Test of Capabilities, Suitability, Tactics and Techniques, and Comparisons of Speedee. (S.T. 1-45-20) AAF Board Project No. F 4480, 10 July 1945. [2] *Ibid*. [3] Final Report, Army Air Forces Board Project No. 4480C471.6, "Test of Capabilities, Suitability, Tactics and Techniques, and Comparisons of 'Speedee,'" 17 July 1945. [4]*Ibid.* [5] *Ibid.* [6] *Ibid.* [7] *Ibid.* [8] *Ibid.* [9] *Ibid.* [10] *Ibid.* [11] *Ibid.*

A-26Bs in training over South Carolina, circa 1945. (Douglas/Harry Gann)

The XA-26F had six internal wing guns and eight fixed nose guns, but the fuselage-mounted jet engine installation deleted both turrets. Beneath the wing, a buzz number uses letters AC to identify this as an A-26, followed by the last three digits of its serial number. When the nomenclature changed, the AC would become BC for the rest of the buzz number era. The sole F-model was photographed 4 June 1946 at Wright Field. (Peter M. Bowers)

FCCTS-5·20·45-G 1176-2-A.P.#41-39420-
A26B.- RESTRICTED.-FL.S.C.

On its nose at Florence, South Carolina, on 20 May 1945, this Invader had both engines turning when the nosewheel collapsed. (Air Force Historical Research Agency)

Clamshell-canopied A-26C (43-22736) was a Florence, South Carolina, casualty on 2 May 1945. (U.S. Air Force)

Shorn of wings, nose, and tail, this A-26B fuselage remained essentially intact during a crash near Harleyville, South Carolina on 29 June 1945. (U.S. Air Force)

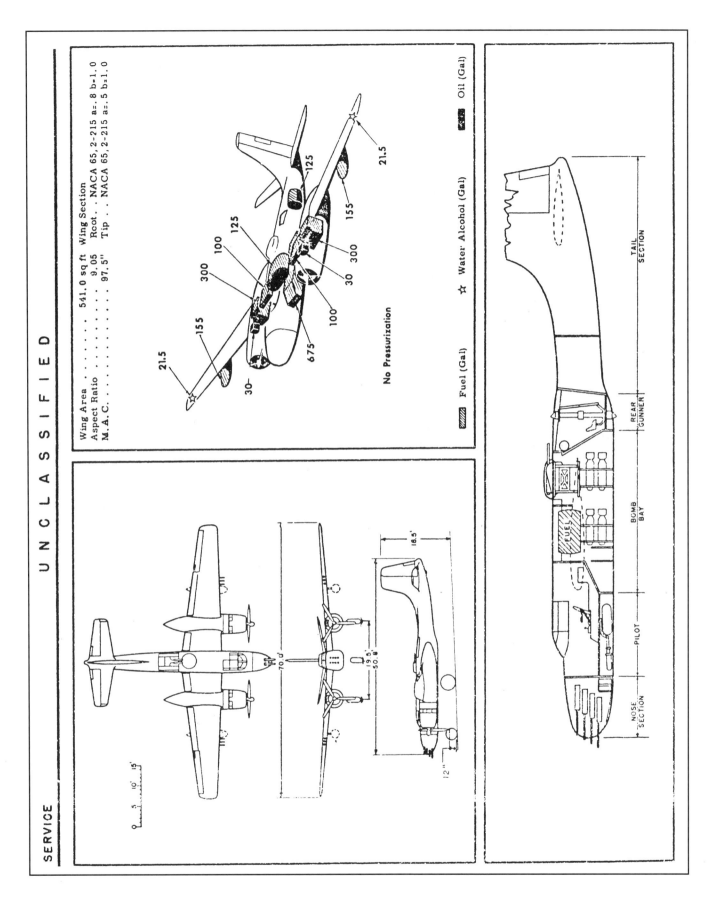

SERVICE

Wing Area . . . . 541.0 sq ft   Wing Section
Aspect Ratio . . . . 9.05   Rcot. . NACA 65, 2-215 a=.8 b=1.0
M.A.C. . . . . 97.5"   Tip . . NACA 65, 2-215 a=.5 b=1.0

No Pressurization

⬡ Fuel (Gal)   ☆ Water Alcohol (Gal)   ▨ Oil (Gal)

TAIL SECTION
REAR GUNNER
BOMB BAY
PILOT
NOSE SECTION

A-26B drawings, for eight-gun nose variant, show flat stowage of nosewheel. Some B-models were not fitted with a ventral turret. (Douglas/Harry Gann)

Olive and gray XA-26, minus tail number, shows how lateral view from the cockpit was blocked by huge engine nacelles, especially on early low-profile canopy A-26s. (Bowers collection)

XA-26A night fighter experiment incorporated a ventral bulge for forward-firing armament. Elongated nose was to carry search radar. When photo was taken, the tail number (42-19505) conflicted with the accepted number for this aircraft (41-19505). (Bowers collection)

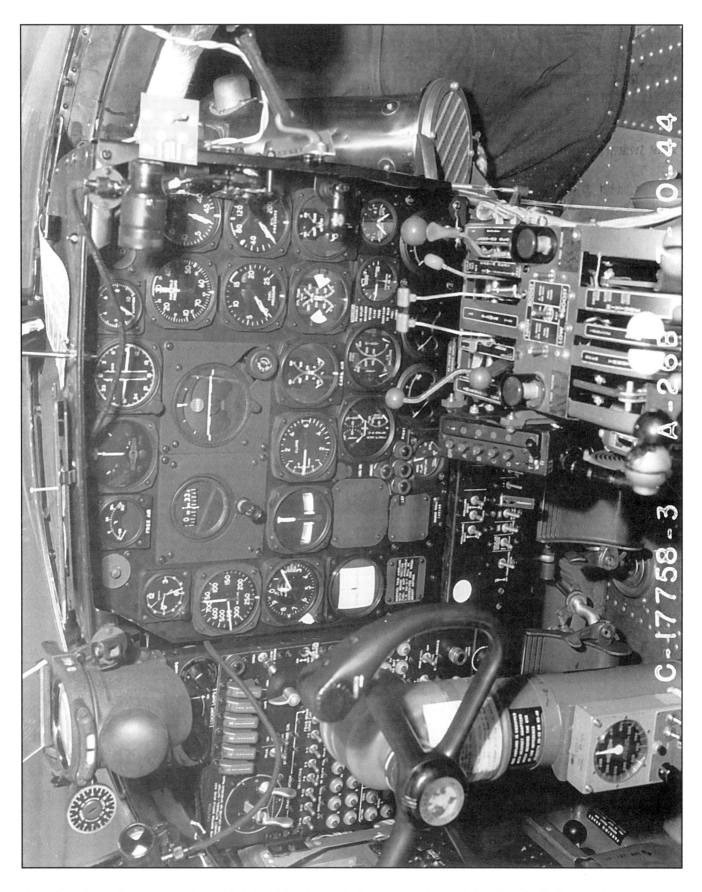

A-26B cockpit photographed on 10 July 1944 showed placement of gunsight ahead of pilot to aid in strafing.
(Douglas)

APPENDIX A

Douglas Invaders flew combat for the United States beginning in 1944 and ending in 1969. As A-26s, then B-26s, and finally A-26s again, these fast, useful bombers equipped many U.S. Army Air Forces, Air Force, and Air National Guard (ANG) squadrons. Some ANG A-26/B-26 units were renumbered iterations of former active duty bomb groups; an effort has been made to list multiple identifications where known, if the unit operated Invaders under more than one organizational identification. American Invader units over the years include:

1st Special Operations Wing: Units in this wing flew A-26s from Hurlburt Field, Florida, circa 1969.

3rd Bomb Group: Flew B-26s from Japan and Korea in Korean War combat, 1950-1953.

10th Reconnaissance Group: Included RB-26s in its complement when operating in Germany in the early 1950s.

12th Bomb Group: Began training on A-26s to replace its B-25s in India in the summer of 1945.

17th Bomb Group: Equipped with B-26s for service in Korean War from mid-1952 until armistice in July 1953, and until replaced with B-57s circa 1955.

38th Bomb Group: Equipped with A-26s in Japan circa 1946; inactivated in 1949, activated again in 1953; assigned to United States Air Forces in Europe (USAFE), initially with B-26s, in 1953.

47th Bomb Group: Served in Mediterranean, receiving some A-26s after January 1945.

56th Special Operations Wing/Air Commando Wing: Flew B-26Ks (A-26As) and other aircraft in Southeast Asia interdiction role in late 1960s.

66th (Tactical) Reconnaissance Group: Flew RB-26s and RF-80s circa 1946-1953, including a stint in Germany.

67th (Tactical) Reconnaissance Group: Equipped with RB-26s and RF-80s in 1947; moved to Korea in March 1951; used RB-26s, RF-51s, RF-80s, RF-86s, and RF-84s.

69th Reconnaissance Group: Trained in the U.S. with A-26s and F-6s in 1945-46; inactivated 29 July 1946.

102nd Bomb Squadron: New York ANG unit, circa 1947-51 and again in 1952-57.

103rd Bomb Squadron: Pennsylvania ANG, circa 1948-51.

106th Bomb Squadron: Alabama ANG, circa 1946-51, B/RB-26.

107th Bomb Squadron: Michigan ANG, circa 1946-50.

108th Bomb Squadron: Illinois ANG, circa 1947-1952.

110th Bomb Squadron: Missouri ANG, 1952-57.

111th Bomb Wing: Relatively short-lived amalgamation of three ANG B-26 squadrons (103rd, 117th, and 122nd Squadrons) circa April 1951; the 117th and 122nd Squadrons subsequently were transferred to Langley AFB, Virginia, to provide B-26 crew training.

112th Bomb Squadron: Ohio ANG, 1946-52.

114th Bomb Squadron: New York ANG, circa 1947-51 and 1952-57.

115th Bomb Squadron: California ANG, 1945-51 and 1952.

117th Bomb Squadron: Pennsylvania ANG, 1948-52.

118th Tactical Reconnaissance Group: ANG unit ordered to active duty in April 1951; operated several aircraft types including RB-26s.

122nd Bomb Squadron: Louisiana ANG, 1946-57.

126th Bomb Wing: Composed of three ANG B-26 squadrons (the 108th, 168th, and 180th) this unit deployed to France in the fall of 1951 to bolster North Atlantic Treaty Organization (NATO) assets.

149th Bomb Squadron: Virginia ANG, circa 1953-58.

155th Squadron: Tennessee ANG, 1953-56, RB-26.

168th Bomb Squadron: Illinois ANG, 1946-57.

180th Bomb Squadron: First Air National Guard (ANG) unit to obtain A-26s as mission aircraft (as opposed to target tug A-26s, which many fighter squadrons in the ANG obtained), 1946-57.

183rd Squadron: Mississippi ANG, 1953-57, RB-26.

184th Squadron: Arkansas ANG, 1953-56, RB-26.

319th Bomb Group: Following Mediterranean service in B-26 Marauders and B-25s, trained with A-26s in 1945 before moving to Okinawa; flew combat strikes to Japan and China.

344th Bomb Group: Began training with A-26s in Europe late in 1945; as ANG (Air National Guard) 126th Bomb Group, used B-26s for training and maneuvers in France circa 1951-52.

345th Bomb Group: When reactivated in 1954, initially equipped with B-26s.

363rd (Tactical) Reconnaissance Group: Activated 29 July 1946; used RF-80s and RB-26s until replaced by RF-84s and RB-57s.

386th Bomb Group: Converted from Marauders to A-26s in time for 1945 combat against Germany.

391st Bomb Group: Converted from Marauders to A-26s in April 1945, flying its last wartime mission against German targets on 3 May. As 111th Bomb Group of ANG, the unit was activated in 1951, assigned to Strategic Air Command, and trained with B-26s and B-29s; later converted to RB-29s.

394th Bomb Group: Began training with A-26s, vice Marauders, in Europe late in 1945.

408th Fighter-Bomber Group: Trained in the U.S. with a variety of aircraft including A-26s circa early 1944.

409th Bomb Group: Converted to A-26s from A-20s by December 1944, attacking German targets.

410th Bomb Group: By February 1945, used an A-26 for target marking during night missions involving A-20s and Marauders as well, against German targets; converted to A-26s too late for combat.

415th Bomb Group: Included some A-26s in its varied fleet used for stateside training and demonstrations of tactics; unit disbanded 5 April 1944.

416th Bomb Group: Converted to A-26s in November 1944; participated in the Battle of the Bulge.

432nd (Tactical) Reconnaissance Group: Operated some RB-26s circa 1954.

452nd Bomb Group: Trained with B-26s circa 1950; used Invaders in Korean War until inactivated there on 10 May 1952.

461st Bomb Group: Trained with B-26s circa 1953-54.

492nd Bomb Group: During March and April 1945, this Carpetbagger organization included the A-26 in its roster of aircraft used for clandestine missions behind German lines.

4400th Combat Crew Training Squadron: Formed in April 1961 to train indigenous air forces in the use of B-26s and other aircraft in counterinsurgency warfare. The unit was nicknamed Jungle Jim.

6167th Operations Squadron (B Flight): Activated 1 April 1952, this unit included some black B-26s at Seoul, South Korea (airfield K-16), for clandestine operations.

(Lists of A-26 units may be found in: Air Force Combat Units of World War II, by Maurer Maurer [Office of Air Force History, 1983]; The Air Guard, by Rene Francillon [Aerofax, 1983]; and individual unit histories maintained by the Air Force Historical Research Agency.)

Tail of a 12th Bomb Group A-26 in India in the late summer of 1945 featured bulldog 82nd Bombardment Squadron insignia. (12th Bomb Group Association)

APPENDIX B

The following is transcribed from a May 1962 price list from On Mark Engineering for civilian conversion of B-26 Invaders.

NOTE: Many of the prices listed below are based on performing the modification at the time of complete aircraft conversion and consequently would be slightly higher if performed separately. Price adjustment would depend on the configuration of the customer's aircraft.

1. Fuselage and spar conversion. Install circumferential rear wing spar. Install airstair door RH side. Install 8 windows (2 picture windows). Recontour fuselage top & bottom. Modify wiring, plumbing, cables, floor, etc. $58,000.

2. Fuselage conversion. Install belly ladder door. Install 8 windows (2 picture windows). Recontour fuselage top only. Modify wiring, plumbing, cables, floor, etc. $38,000.

3. Custom Interior. $17,000.

4. Deluxe Interior. $25,000.

5. Install Wing Tip Tanks (165 gal. each). Modify wing, plumbing and valves. Install boost pumps and dump valves. $16,710.

6. Install Pliocell Wing Tanks (100 gallons each). Modify wing, plumbing and valves. $10,500.

7. Replace existing self-sealing main and aux. fuel tanks with lightweight Pliocell tanks. (reduces airplane weight 450 lbs.) $5,200. With top filler necks (adds 90 gal. usable fuel). Includes A.D. Note compliance. $6,000.

8. Install 103" Plastic Nose. Includes ladder baggage door. Provides for 1,000 lbs. baggage and radar. $10,500.

9. Install dual controls. $5,500.

10. Install Co-Pilot Brake Pedals. $990.

11. Install 100,000 B.T.U. Heater and Ducting. $3,900.

12. Install Custom Instrument Panel. Includes complete set flight instruments for co-pilot. Includes custom glare shield for radio controls. $4,250.

13. Install Scott High Pressure Oxygen System. $1,800.

14. Install DC-6 Wheels and Brakes. $4,850. In kit form. $4,450.

15. Install Hytrol Anti-skid braking system. $5,250.

16. Chrome Plate landing Gear struts. $1,200.

17. Install Tip Tank Landing Lights. $1,050.

18. Install De-icer Boots all Surfaces. (Goodrich high-pressure "stick-on" type) $8,850.

19. Install Long all-metal rudder. Includes modified tail cone and vortex generators. $9,750.

20. Install Nose Wheel Steering. Choice of rudder pedal or aux. wheel control. $1,995. In kit form $1,550.

21. "Ceconite" covered Control Surfaces—exchange. $1,800. With new draft curtains $2,150. Installed complete $2,450.

22. Modify Canopy. Metalized top and install double glass $1,750.

23. Modify Cockpit Plumbing and Structure. Provide space for observer seat $3,100.

24. Install Refrigerated Air Conditioning. Operates in flight or on the ground $5,000.

25. Install Auxiliary Power Unit: New 105 ampere Homelite APU $2,450. Surplus 70 ampere APU $1,700.

26. Custom Exterior Paint—paint only. $3,850. Strip and clean $960. Seal Exterior $1,100.

27. Install 20-gallon Engine Alcohol Tank. $870.

28. Install Fire Warning and Fire Extinguishing System with

Firewall Shut-off Valves. $2,650.

29. Install Modified Short Metal Nose. Includes ladder baggage door. $2,500.

30. Install New Bendix Weather Radar. Includes Sperry Gyro Antenna Stabilization (103" Plastic nose required) $18,500.

31. Install Overhauled, Certified Sperry A-12 Autopilot unit $18,500.

32. Install P&W R-2800 "C" Series engines with Hamilton Standard 33E60 High-activity pro- pellers and autofeather. Labor and installation material only. Engines and propellers priced separately. $15,450.

33. Install P&W R-2800 "CB" Series engines with Hamilton Standard 33E60 High-activity propellers and autofeather. Labor and installation material only. Engines and propellers priced separately. Includes ADI installation. $16,800.

34. Install propeller spinners and afterbodies. Includes cowling mod. for inside carb. air scoops. On request.

35. Install Hamilton Standard 43E60 reversing propellers on "C" or "CB" engines. Labor and installation material only. Propellers priced separately. $4,800.

36. Install Booster Tab Rudder and Vortex Generators (with exchange rudder). Lowers Vmc to 118 mph C.A.S. (standard engines). Includes new Ceconite cover and matching paint $3,950. In kit form $3,750.

37. Flap modification for increased flap extension speed. 25 degrees flaps may be extended at 250 mph I.A.S. $265. In kit form $145.

The Diamond Match corporate On Mark conversion included metalized canopy hatches, as seen in an On Mark photo taken in February 1957. (San Diego Aerospace Museum)

SIGNIFICANT DATES

November 1940
Air Corps Experimental Engineering Section gave first priority to Douglas to design a replacement for the A-20, that might also replace the B-25 and Martin B-26.

2 June 1941
Contract W535 ac-17946 signed for one XA-26 and one XA-26A night fighter; almost immediately, a change order added a 75-mm cannon-firing XA-26B variant.

31 October 1941
First mass-production contract (ac-21393) approved, for 500 A-26s, for a total of $78,264,093.

10 July 1942
First flight of XA-26.

July 1944
Four A-26s given combat tests in Fifth Air Force.

December 1944
Schedule called for delivery by the end of the month of the first production variant to have the revised raised cockpit canopy for greater visibility.

June 1948
Air Force eliminated attack bomber designations; with Martin B-26 Marauders no longer in U.S. service, A-26s were redesignated B-26s, causing a continuing unintended confusion between the two twin-engine bomber types.

27/28 June 1950
Third Bomb Group began Korean War tactical intruder sorties with B-26s out of Iwakuni AB, Japan.

15-19 April 1961
B-26s flown by Cuban expatriates and American volunteers attacked airfield targets near the Bay of Pigs as part of an invasion of Cuba that failed.

28 January 1963
First flight of YB-26K Counter Invader.

3 February 1963
Viet Cong gunners downed a Farm Gate RB-26, killing American Capts. John F. Shaughnessy, Jr., and John P. Bartley, underscoring early U.S. involvement in the war in Vietnam.

November 1963
On Mark Engineering of Van Nuys, Calif., received USAF contract to modify 40 B-26s to K-model Counter Invader configuration.

March 1964
End of combat operations by B-26s of First Air Commando Squadron (Farm Gate) in Vietnam precipitated by wing fatigue.

25 May 1964
First flight of a production B-26K.

August 1964
Three newly shopped B-26K Counter Invaders delivered to Congo for combat.

23 October 1969
A-26s of the 603rd Special Operations Squadron (SOS) departed Hurlburt Field, Florida, for retirement to the storage facility at Davis-Monthan AFB, Arizona.

30 June 1970
Closeout of the A/B-26 Invader as a USAF logistics/support item by the Ogden Air Materiel Area.

7 December 1977
Final flight of Indonesian B-26B I.D. number M-265; this may have been last fully armed Invader in military service anywhere.

Two B-26s of the 17th Bomb Group over Korea show the grime of heavy use. Aircraft nearest camera is Bob Mikesh's Monie. (Courtesy Robert C. Mikesh)